SpringerBriefs in Economics

SpringerBriefs present concise summaries of cutting-edge research and practical applications across a wide spectrum of fields. Featuring compact volumes of 50 to 125 pages, the series covers a range of content from professional to academic. Typical topics might include:

- A timely report of state-of-the art analytical techniques
- A bridge between new research results, as published in journal articles, and a contextual literature review
- A snapshot of a hot or emerging topic
- An in-depth case study or clinical example
- A presentation of core concepts that students must understand in order to make independent contributions

SpringerBriefs in Economics showcase emerging theory, empirical research, and practical application in microeconomics, macroeconomics, economic policy, public finance, econometrics, regional science, and related fields, from a global author community.
Briefs are characterized by fast, global electronic dissemination, standard publishing contracts, standardized manuscript preparation and formatting guidelines, and expedited production schedules.

More information about this series at http://www.springer.com/series/8876

Dagmara Nikulin • Ewa Lechman

Shadow Economy in Poland

Recent Evidence Based on Survey Data

Springer

Dagmara Nikulin
Faculty of Management and Economics
Gdańsk University of Technology
Gdansk, Poland

Ewa Lechman
Faculty of Management and Economics
Gdańsk University of Technology
Gdansk, Poland

ISSN 2191-5504 ISSN 2191-5512 (electronic)
SpringerBriefs in Economics
ISBN 978-3-030-70523-7 ISBN 978-3-030-70524-4 (eBook)
https://doi.org/10.1007/978-3-030-70524-4

This Springer imprint is published by the registered company Springer Nature Switzerland AG
The registered company address is: Gewerbestrasse 11, 6330 Cham, Switzerland

Foreword

The shadow economy includes not only paid transactions not declared to the authorities for the purposes of evading tax, social security and labour laws but also criminal activities where the provision of the goods and services that are themselves unlawful (e.g., the production or trafficking of illegal drugs, human trafficking or money laundering forbidden by law). In recent years, this has become a priority for action of both supra-national institutions such as the ILO, European Commission, OECD and World Bank, but also for national governments.

The reason it has become a focus of attention is due to its negative impacts on workers, businesses and the wider society. Workers in the shadow economy lack legal protection and suffer poorer working conditions, legitimate enterprises suffer unfair competition and governments lose tax revenue and regulatory control over working conditions, which limits their ability to pursue social inclusion.

Contrary to popular opinion, this is not just a problem of the developing world. It is also a pervasive phenomenon in advanced and transition economies. This book captures that fact. It displays how in Poland the shadow economy is an extensive phenomenon that pervades many aspects of everyday life. As this book recognises, however, there is no point in just mapping its size. If it is to be tackled, there is a need to understand what causes its existence. Unless these causes are known and understood, then policies are in danger of being developed that either do not deal with its root causes or which simply deal with the effects rather than the determinants.

Through detailed empirical evidence this book unpicks the key determinants of the shadow economy in Poland and starts to unpick what needs to be done to address this problem. The findings regarding both determinants and solutions are potentially transferable to many other countries. There have been so far too few detailed studies of the shadow economy across the world. This book starts to fill that gap. Given that the International Labour Organisation estimates that more than 60% of the global labour force have their main employment in this sphere, this book holds many lessons not only for Poland but also the wider world.

University of Sheffield
Sheffield, UK

Colin C. Williams,

Foreword

Acknowledgements

This book is an effect of the merit cooperation on the shadow economy between Gdansk University of Technology Faculty of Management and Economics and Stockholm Business School in Riga (Prof. Arnis Sauka).

In Poland the survey research has been financed by Gdansk University of Technology Faculty of Management and Economics internal grant.

Contents

Chapter 1
Introductory Words

"Any economic system in the world (…) is a unique synthesis of legal and illegal-shadow economic activities. (…) The shadow economy as a phenomenon originated in ancient times and functions 'successfully' up to the present, at a time when its scale is not only expanding in practice but also assumes myriad forms"

Papava and Khaduri (1997) in "On the shadow political economy of the post-communist transformation: An institutional analysis" Problems of Economic Transition, 40(6), p. 15.

Abstract This introductory chapter sets the general context and background in regard to shadow economy. It briefly explains its merit and defines as a problem that economies are facing. This chapter additionally presents the structure of the book, its major aims and scopes and also shows Poland as a transition economy, which is of central interest in the empirical part of this work.

1.1 To Begin

This book is dedicated to Poland, Central-Eastern European transition economy, which in 1989 began its shock therapy to transit from centrally-planed ineffective and corrupted economy to free and market-based one. Before 1989 in Poland, but also in all countries of the so called Soviet Block, the existence of unofficial, parallel economic system was natural and allowed compensating multiple shortcomings of centrally-planed state. To a large extent, it was tolerated by official authorities and it has quasi-legal status (Dubova & Kosal's, 2013; Huber, 1985). Still, existing peculiarities of soviet economies that enhanced enormous increases of informal economic activities, were something different than in e.g. Western countries. Interestingly, even the collapse of the Soviet Block, did not liquidated the problem

D. Nikulin, E. Lechman, *Shadow Economy in Poland*, SpringerBriefs in Economics, https://doi.org/10.1007/978-3-030-70524-4_1

of extensive shadow economy, but—reversely, profound and rapid structural changes even aggravated it. Since 1989 onward, in all post-Soviet economies, including Poland, the shadow economy boosted, which to a large extend was a negative consequence of poor official institutions and weak enforcement of laws and protection of property rights, administrative burdens, inefficient bureaucracy and costly procedures, low probability of being caught as an illicit worker, and broad acceptance of illicit work, overwhelming corruption, high structural unemployment, high propensity to get corrupted, low tax morale. Today, in 2020, the situation has radically changed. The massiveness of the unreported economic activities is gradually dropping and post-Soviet countries are doing much better in fighting against unreported activities.

1.2 Setting the Context

Josef Huber in his paper "Concepts of dual economy" (Huber, 1985) presents a short glossary of the dual economy, claiming that the emergence of *"a conceptual "tuttifrutti" which leads to political hodgepodge, if it leads anywhere at all"* (Huber, 1985, p. 1). He also writes between 1920s and 1970s the term "mixed economy" was broadly used in literature, however growing interests of both academics, practitioners and politicians resulted in fast growing number of terms aiming to describe the "past mixed economy". Huber traced 19 different terms labelling the "mixed economy": informal sector, shadow economy, hidden economy, invisible economy, illegal sector, underground economy, counter-economy, parallel economy, secondary economy, non-registered economy, black market, non-market sector, autonomous sector, voluntary sector, self-help sector, community sector, neighbourhood economy, shadow work, vernacular sphere (Huber, 1985).

Today, informal (shadow) economy remains one of the major structural problems to be challenged across economies worldwide (Williams & Schneider, 2016). Both existence and the size of the informal sector negatively affects functioning of the national economy; it violates fair competition among companies, slows down productivity shifts, generates hidden unemployment and financial (fiscal) loses to state budgets, which hampers stable long-term economic growth and development. Needless to underline that expansion of undeclared economy may drive the emergence of a destructive cycle meaning that transaction done in the shadow economy—by definition, escape taxation, which keeps state tax revenues lower than would be. This may induce tax raises driving further escapes into shadow economy (Schneider & Enste, 2013). Various studies unveil different reasons why people stay 'in the shadow'. For instance reading work of Schneider and Enste (2013) we learn that in well-developed and highly industrialized economies factors that drive the emergence of undeclared work are tax burden, too high social security contributions, weak tax morale and—to some extent, corruption in public institutions, intensity of legal regulations especially with respect to labour market. In seeking to understand the shadow economy its multiple aspects shall be borne in mind. On very general level it is seminal to know, at least partially, to what extend shadow economy activities distort official national statistics on fundamental macroeconomic variables like for instance gross national output, inflation or employment. Extensive shadow economy may be claimed as one of the free-market failure, which emergence if enforce by unfriendly legal regulations, extensive tax burden and low tax morale, high labor costs imposed on employers, or simply weak national institutions. To some extend examining the size of the shadow economy is also important from a different angle—it allows us understanding how extensive government policy shapes both individuals and enterprises market behaviour. On the other hand empirical research on the shadow economy is extremely difficult, since we have only limited access to the relevant data. The major obstacles stem from the fact that those who work informally or run informal business will protect their anonymity. Moreover, informality can take many shapes: there are workers with a second informal job whose main job is formal, those receiving a part of their remuneration as unregistered, workers involved solely in the informal sector or informal workers who are not allowed to work legally (such as immigrants) (Schneider, 2002a). Main motive for operating in informal markets is the tax evasion which may pose different possibilities both legally and unlawfully.

Despite the fact, that generally shadow economy activities generate more economic losses than gains, arguably, when considering transition economies, such 'unreported' activities have helped their transition from state-led to free market economies. This is mainly because it might have helped them to mobilize previously unused recourses—especially labor force, enhance entrepreneurial endeavor and attitudes. We might even raise claims that shadow economy activities are to some point stimulating official economic activity mainly due to growing aggregate demand. Needless to explain that incomes earned in unofficial economy are directly 'transferred' to formal economy and may rise aggregate supply and thus national output. Extensive shadow economy may additionally constitute a sever impediment for developing registered (legal) enterprise, which in turn may determine growth of the tax rates to cover budget deficits and thus constitute another sever impediment for dynamic development of the legal business. This in turn limits the government's possibilities to provide public goods, invest in infrastructure, educational and health care system; henceforth the whole economy suffers from due to lack of public financial resources. In the longer-run perspective this may constitute an important obstacle for economic growth and development. Put shortly, extensive shadow economy may be generated by ineffective and complicated taxation systems, high tax evasion, minimum wages or low quality of institutions. In effect tax revenues fall and thus budget deficits growth.

The shadow economy is the cash-based economy and it is predominantly generated in the sector of micro and small enterprises as they constitute more than 90% of total firm's population. These two are strictly related to each other. Micro and small enterprises operate only in certain branches; many of them operate in rural areas where it is relatively easy to hide employment and run unregistered economic activity. Another important issue, often raised when discussing the shadow economy, is the fact that its existence heavily violates cross-companies free-market competition. Paradoxically, companies operating in the shadow they usually results to be far more competitive than those that run their business fully legally. It is mainly possible because of tax avoidance, which enable the 'shadow enterprises' to offer their goods and services at lower prices, which makes then automatically more competitive. The size of the shadow strongly correlates with phase of the business cycle. During the recession phase fewer opportunities to find job, lower disposable income, thus individuals tend to drift to the 'shadow activities'. During the contraction phase of the business cycle, when individuals` personal income do not grow or even drop, and thus people's propensity to buy cheap items intensifies. Additionally, during the recession phase of the business cycle, those companies that until now where legally operating tend to move to the 'shadow' to avoid bankruptcy. As due to the existence of the 'shadow economy' free-market competition mechanisms are violated, it may lead to the situation when prices becomes the only factor that determines firm's competitive position. Henceforth, it is the price itself instead of e.g. innovativeness, which is decisive for wining market competition. The latter however, lower the pressure to innovate and increase productivity and thus results in economic losses. Interestingly, from the pure economic perspective profits generate in the shadow economy may be claimed as a kind of risk premium (Çiçek & Elgin, 2011; Jung, Snow, & Trandel, 1994).

1.3 Why Poland?

Following data provided in Global Entrepreneurship Monitor 2014 Poland is claimed a country with intensively growing entrepreneurial sector, while the growth of number small and medium sized enterprises is especially visible. In GEM 2014 it is clearly stated that year 2014 in Poland a seminal increase was noted in respect to the relationship between opportunity-, and necessity-driven entrepreneurship. The push-type factors impeding entrepreneurial activity was determined by relatively slow changing educational structure and low-quality of work, which—in effect, due to high unemployment rates forced people to set up their own business. Among the pull-type factors a high pressure for 'going abroad' and start export activities was observed, growing international competition and rent-seeking behavior, economic policies incentives for setting up new businesses. However, dynamic development of free entrepreneurship and substantial growth of enterprise population was—unfortunately, accompanied by fast growth of the shadow economy.

Since late 1980s onward, Central and Eastern European economies have been profoundly transforming in various aspects. Also, since early 90s of twentieth century Poland has been undergoing extensive political, institutional and structural shifts, which resulted in the emergence of multiple positive, but also some negative effects. Political and economic transformation in Poland generated extensive changes in entrepreneurship sector. One very important and decisive trend in enhancing entrepreneurship development in post communists countries was moving from state-controlled economy to free-market-based economy. Along with the latter, all of these economies have actively undertaken public policies to promote entrepreneurship, as one of the major channels of boosting economic growth and development. Poland, as transition economy, is widely recognized as one of the most dynamically developing country in Central-Eastern Europe. Still, growth of new companies is preconditioned by entrepreneurial skills to carry business functions effectively; henceforth since mid-1990s, Polish government has undertaken multiple efforts towards improvement of entrepreneurial skills and attitudes, creating firm-friendly environment has been effective enough, so that now in Poland SMEs contribution to national economy—both in terms value added creation and employment, is steadily growing. In Global Entrepreneurship Monitor from 2014 we read that in Poland there was also an important change regarding the relationship between opportunity-, and necessity driven entrepreneurship, and the first was reported as of relatively higher importance. Positive changes along with profound institutional reforms promoting new firms creation, significant shifts in terms of R&D, providing solid foundations for financial and capital markets emergence allowing for various sources of rising financial capital for investments undoubtedly contributed significantly to increasing 'quality' of entrepreneurship in Poland. However, although multiple positive changes that are easily observed in Poland, the socio-economic cost of those shifts is high and may be seen through the lens of—for instance, extensive shadow economy, which boosted in early 90s of twentieth century. Regarding the phenomenon of undeclared work—as socio-economic and political problem, Poland, as post-communist and transition economy seems to be a perfect location to study the problem of the shadow economy, both in terms of its extent and determinants. In Poland, the shadow economy still remains relatively poorly explored field of study. The empirical evidence both on the extent and determinants of the shadow economy in Poland is fragmented and scattered. From few works tackling these aspects, we learn that at the beginning of transformation the size of undeclared work in Poland was extensive, which was a direct negative consequence of profound structural changes that polish economy was undergoing. In Lackó (1999) we find estimates showing that in 1991 the size of the shadow economy achieved 33% of national GDP. In consecutive 2 years it was dropping by 1% p.p. annually, then in 1994 it was 28% and in 1995—24%. It also shall be borne in mind that authors use different methods to estimate the size of the shadow economy, which—obviously—produces different results. The most commonly used methods are the MIMIC method[1] (see Buehn & Schneider, 2013), calculations based on the National Accounts Discrepancy method for Non-Observed Economy (NOE) (see, e.g. Gyomai & van de Ven, 2014), survey-based methods—see, for instance, some data used from Special Eurobarometer survey No. 402, or Enterprise Surveys run by the World Bank. Regarding Poland, MIMIC method (on macro level) to estimate the shadow economy size was used by Schneider (2016) who reported for 2003—27.7%, and then for 2012—24.7% of unreported activities; while when using

[1] The MIMIC method—multiple indicator multiple cause method assumes that shadow economy is the unobservable variables that is simply estimated based on various quantifiable causes of the shadow economy, as well as indicators of illicit activity.

adjusted-corrected MIMIC method Schneider finds that unreported activities are just 16% of the total economy (Schneider, 2017) and similar estimates are reported by OECD applying National Accounts estimates of NOE[2] for 2011 and 2012. While when referring more to micro level estimates provided using Eurobarometer 2013 data (European Commission, 2014) we see that—according to surveys results, envelope wages constitute 5% of the total wages paid, people employed without formal contract are just 2%. These results however contradict with those obtained using macro-level methods. Then when results from World Bank Enterprise Survey 2013 (http://www.enterprisesurveys.org), suggest indirectly the extent of the problem of the shadow economy—it claims that barely 30% of firms compete against unregistered or informal firms, and slightly above 15% of companies identifies practices of their competitors in the informal sector as a major constrain in doing their business. In Poland, so far, some attempts to estimate the size of the of informal economy, has been done by Statistics Poland[3] that combine the legal but not registered part of economic activities and its estimates based on data gathered from Labour Force Survey and The Module Survey Unregistered Employment (MSUE). Along with the latter, they occasionally estimate share of workers in shadow economy in total employment, and additional estimates are done using The Module Survey Unregistered Employment where unregistered employment is measured as the share of the total number of people employed. Different estimates are provided by Gdansk Institute for Market Economics (IBnGR), which so far has presented estimates of the shadow economy for the period 2011–2016. IBnGR aside the hidden but legal activities also include illegal activities, which by definition stay in the 'shadow'. Still, needles to emphasize that in Poland between 1990 and 2020, dynamic development of free entrepreneurship and substantial growth of enterprise population was—unfortunately, accompanied by fast growth of the shadow economy. This negative process negatively affects the long-run economic development, and thus we claim that identifying major determinants of the latter is essential. To stay in line with the latter, the empirical part of the paper is entirely dedicated to discussing our findings—that base on firm-level surveys, regarding these elements that push entrepreneurs to undertake undeclared economic activities.

1.4 Aims and Scopes

Having in mind the above, this study is dedicated to the issue of shadow economy in Poland. Current state of research indicates rather poor and unsatisfied exploration in this area, mainly due to the lack if relevant data. This research was designed to address two major targets. First, using data collected from firm-level survey, we aim to estimate the size of the shadow economy in Poland. Second, using analogous

[2] National Accounts Discrepancy method for Non-Observed Economy.

[3] National Central Statistical Office.

data, we target to trace core determinants of the existence of the shadow economy in Poland. More specifically, we aimed to find the evidence on

- entrepreneurs opinions on general satisfaction with business climate in Poland;
- degree of misreporting declared by interviewed entrepreneurs;
- opinion on perceived probability of being caught on misreporting and possible penalties;
- feelings on belonging to local community.

To examine the determinants of shadow economy, we draw on an enterprise survey conducted in Poland in April 2017. The study was carried out on behalf on the Faculty of Management and Economics, Gdańsk University of Technology in Poland by the data collecting company Tomasz Czuba MRC Consulting. The survey was run for 454 representative polish enterprises was interviewed using the he telephone interviews (CATI) with the company owners or high level managers. The survey‘s main purpose is to explore the entrepreneurs' satisfaction with entrepreneurship climate in Poland. The questionnaire form as well as general the methodology was developed using the survey conducted in Baltic states since 2010 by Putniņš and Sauka (2015) and it was composed of 23 questions divided into four sections: external influences, government policy and amount of informal business, company performance and attitudes towards informal economy and barriers to business. In particular, we employed the tools typical for sensitive questions survey, implemented among others in BEEPS as well as in Putniņš and Sauka research on Baltic states. We are aware of the bias related to the survey study. However, as the questions are asked not directly and concern the assessment of shadow activities in companies in the industry, the probability of getting untrue answers is minimized.

The representativeness of the results is ensured by using stratified sample with following strata: region (voivodship), industry and employment size. Most of the companies are micro enterprises with fewer than ten employees (95.81% of all surveyed companies). Moreover, the majority of interviewed company is younger than 20 years (84.38% of companies was established after 1998) and 33.33% of them have fewer than 10 years. Analysing the sector in which the main activity is performed, the bulk of companies are active in service sector (48.85%), manufacturing (19.82%), retail (13.21%), construction (11.41%) and wholesale (5.71%). Since the sample is representative for the whole country, it covers all voivodships. The regional diversity of shadow activities in Poland was taken into account at the stage of survey study design and survey frame construction. As are data are representative for the whole economy (through the process of stratification) we are entitled to apply the results on the national level. The spatial distribution of interviewed companies reflects the proportion of enterprises in given voivodships and is as follows: Masovia (17.42% of all interviewed companies), Greater Poland (11.11%), Silesia (10.21%), Kujavia-Pomerania (8.71%), Lower Silesia, Lesser Poland and Łódź (7.51%), West Pomerania (5.71%), Lublin (4.5%), Lubusz, Opole, Subcarpathia, Pomerania and Warmia-Masuria (3.6%), Holy Cross Province (1.5%) and Podlaskie (0.3%).

1.5 The Structure

This book comprises Preface, four logically structured chapters and Appendix. The first Chapter is the introduction, it sets the general context of the study. **Chapter 1** explains the contents of the consecutive chapters, defines major aims and scopes of the empirical part, explains data collection procedures and briefly discusses seminal findings of this research. **Chapter 2** broadens the context of this study, extensively discusses its background and motivation. In Chap. 2 we present a brief discussion of how shadow economy is defined in world literature. We refer to contributing works of, *inter alia*, Schneider (1997, 2002b, 2005), Schneider, Khan, Hamid, and Khan (2019), Williams and Schneider (2013). In this part of the book, we additionally intend to capture the socio-economic and institutional factors as elements that may significantly precondition not only the existence of the Shadow Economy as such, but also its size and over time persistence. This part of the book yields answering—at least partially, what are the potential economic consequences of extensive Shadow Economy; whether it has "good or bad" impact on economic growth and development. We stress that multidimensional nature of this phenomena makes it even more difficult to explore, quantify and trace its direct causes. It show that the Shadow Economy issues have various contextual dimensions (Sauka & Schneider, 2016), which vary between countries, regions, branches and industries. Next, **Chap. 3** concentrates on two major issues; it shows how shadow economy is measured and traces past empirical evidence in this regard. In this part of the book we plan to include the brief summary and description of different methods used to estimate the size of shadow economy. This can be done mostly using past empirical research. Implementing such comparisons, reviews may be useful and add to our broader understanding of the problem. This additional discussion might also demonstrate some advantages and disadvantages of specific methods usage to estimate the size of shadow economy. Notably, especially interesting and valuable would be presentation of methods that use macro-, versus micro-approach. The materials proposed for the Chap. 3 also constitute perfect fundaments for cross-country comparisons, both of the size, direct and indirect determinants of the Shadow Economy. It also provides solid background for presented empirical evidence for Poland, presented and discussed in consecutive Chapters. Next Chaps. 4 and 5 are entirely empirical and presents our findings on the size and determinants of the Shadow Economy in Poland. First part of **Chap. 4** is entirely devoted to explanation of the data and research methods used in our research. Indeed, in general the methodology used in the survey study follows the method developed by Putniņš and Sauka (2015). In particular, we employed the tools typical for sensitive questions survey, implemented among others in BEEPS as well as in Putniņš and Sauka research on Baltic states. The detailed description of the methods will be provided in the brief. Next, in Chap. 4, we present and discuss the results of our empirical study. Using data collected from firm-level survey, we show estimates of the size of the shadow economy in Poland. With this aim we use visualization and statistical techniques, which facilitate concluding on the size of the Shadow Economy in Poland. Moreover, we aim to compare our results with analogous for neighbouring countries, and—if possible, remaining Central-Eastern economies for which adequate data are available. Such cross-country comparisons would enrich the study and allowed showing our results in broader perspective. Consecutive empirical part is designed to identify major causes of the existence and the size of the Shadow Economy and Poland. We target to trace core determinants of the existence of the shadow economy in Poland, and with this aim we plan to use econometric modelling, like binary outcome models, as well as descriptive analysis of potential factors. In the discussion, we add more context—social, economic, institutional, for the whole study as for the answer received from the companies surveyed. Moreover, we interpret our results on the Shadow Economy determinants in the context of the regional diversity of shadow activities in Poland, legal framework, structure of the national economy, labor markets regulation and social norms and attitudes. Finally, **Chap. 5** draws major conclusion and policy recommendations.

References

Buehn, A., & Schneider, F. (2013). A preliminary attempt to estimate the financial flows of transnational crime using the MIMIC method. In *Research handbook on money laundering*. Cheltenham: Edward Elgar Publishing.

Çiçek, D., & Elgin, C. (2011). Cyclicality of fiscal policy and the shadow economy. *Empirical Economics, 41*(3), 725–737.

Dubova, A., & Kosal's, L. (2013). Russian police involvement in the shadow economy. *Russian Politics & Law, 51*(4), 48–58.

European Commission. (2014). *Undeclared work in the European Union. Special Eurobarometer 402.*

Gyomai, G., & van de Ven, P. (2014). The non-observed economy in the system of national accounts. *OECD Statistics Brief.*

Huber, J. (1985). Conceptions of the dual economy. *Technological Forecasting and Social Change, 27*(1), 63–73.

Jung, Y. H., Snow, A., & Trandel, G. A. (1994). Tax evasion and the size of the underground economy. *Journal of Public Economics, 54*(3), 391–402.

Lackó, M. (1999). *Do power consumption data tell the story?—Electricity intensity and hidden economy in post-socialist countries* (No. BWP-1999/2). Budapest Working Papers on the Labour Market.

Papava, V., & Khaduri, N. (1997). On the shadow political economy of the post-communist transformation: An institutional analysis. *Problems of Economic Transition, 40*(6), 15–34.

Putniņš, T. J., & Sauka, A. (2015). Measuring the shadow economy using company managers. *Journal of Comparative Economics, 43*(2), 471–490. https://doi.org/10.1016/j.jce.2014.04.001

Sauka, A., & Schneider, F. (Eds.). (2016). *Entrepreneurship and the shadow economy*. Edward Elgar Publishing.

Schneider, F. (1997). The shadow economies of Western Europe. *Journal of the Institute of Economic Affairs, 17*(3), 42–48.

Schneider, F. (2002a). Size and measurement of the informal economy in 110 countries. In *Workshop of Australian National Tax Centre*. Canberra: ANU.

Schneider, F. G. (2002b). *The size and development of the shadow economies of 22 transition and 21 OECD countries* (IZA Discussion Papers, No. 514). Bonn: Institute for the Study of Labor (IZA).

Schneider, F. (2005). Shadow economies around the world: What do we really know? *European Journal of Political Economy, 21*(4), 598–642.

Schneider, F. (2016). *Size and development of the shadow economy of 31 European and 5 other OECD countries from 2003 to 2012: Some new facts.* http://www.econ.jku.at/members/Schneider/files/publications/2012/ShadEcEurope31.pdf. Retrieved February, from http://www.econ.jku.at/schneider

Schneider, F. (2017). *Implausible large differences of the size of the underground economies in highly developed European countries? A comparison of different estimation methods* (CESifo Working Paper No. 6522).

Schneider, F., & Enste, D. H. (2013). *The shadow economy: An international survey*. Cambridge University Press.

Schneider, F., Khan, S., Hamid, B. A., & Khan, A. (2019). *Does the tax undermine the effect of remittances on shadow economy*? (Economics Discussion Papers, No 2019-67). Kiel Institute for the World Economy. Received October 20, from http://www.economics-ejournal.org/economics/discussionpapers/2019-67

Williams, C. C., & Schneider, F. (2013). *The shadow economy*. London: Institute of Economic Affairs.

Williams, C. C., & Schneider, F. (2016). *Measuring the global shadow economy: The prevalence of informal work and labour*. Edward Elgar Publishing.

Chapter 2
Shadow Economy: Setting the Economic and Institutional Context

"When I estimated the total 1976 U.S. subterranean economy in the Nov./Dec. 1977 Financial Analysts Journal 1, a conservative figure of somewhat over 10 per cent of official output, tremendous interest ensued. Today, it is widely recognized with many aliases: underground, black, irregular, shadow, unofficial, hidden, unrecorded, parallel, informal, submerged, clandestine, unobserved, concealed, dual, cash, twilight, moonlight, second economy, counter economy and the back door. It is called fiddling, l'economia sommersa, Schwarzarbeit, travail aunoir, Schattenwirtschaft, lavaro nero and morocho"

Peter M. Gutmann in Studies in Contemporary Economics, The Economics of the Shadow Economy Proceedings of the International Conference on the Economics of the Shadow Economy Held at the University of Bielefeld, West Germany October 10–14,1983, Wulf Gaertner and Alois Wenig (eds).

Abstract This chapter sets some conceptual views on the shadow economy as such. It discusses major theoretical and conceptual approaches to the notion of the shadow economy; it explains its consequences for the whole national economy. It briefly shows major characteristics of the shadow economy in developing, developed and transition economies, and it also intends to trace major causes of the shadow economy. Finally it synthetizes several past empirical evidences on the determinants of the shadow economy in Poland.

D. Nikulin, E. Lechman, *Shadow Economy in Poland*, SpringerBriefs in Economics, https://doi.org/10.1007/978-3-030-70524-4_2

2.1 Shadow Economy

Shadow economy,[1] also labelled parallel or dual economy, unobserved sector, subterranean economy is one of the free market failure. The existence of undeclared (unreported), unused labor force affects the functioning of the whole economy through different channels of impact. By some undeclared economic activities are perceived as a demonstration of entrepreneurial talent and creativity, and by others as "cushion" during the crises and recession times that allows escaping unemployment and bankruptcies. On one hand, extensive shadow labor market can argued one of the effects of ineffective state, weak institutions, lack of effective and adequate legal frameworks, overwhelming corruption and weakly functioning markets; while on the other hand its society-, and economy-wide negative consequences are sever and far-reaching. Major negative consequences of shadow economy are breakdowns and losses in state taxation system, misleading and erroneous "official" statistics that lead governments to take inadequate decisions and strategies, growing labor force but also small business dependency on activities undertaken in the shadow, increasing labor force vulnerability and external risk exposure; while among the most common causes of shadow economy, issues such as extensive tax burdens and extensive governmental regulations or prohibition of certain activities are cited. Still, the short list above is by no means exhaustive. However, regardless of its root causes and socio-economic consequences, informal economy captures a significant share of global labor force that remains outside formal statistics, outside formal world, and outside stable and law-protected employment, which constitutes a problem *sensu stricte*.

The history of the shadow economy is relatively short. Since its "discovery" in 1970s (Chen & Carré, 2020) and contributing work of Allingham and Sandmo (1972) on income tax evasion that provides conceptual and theoretical foundation for further discussion on shadow economy, we observe growing attention to the problem in academic world. One of the first studies dealing with issues of informal economy is that of Keith Hart (1973) on "Informal income opportunities and urban employment in Ghana" and published in *The journal of modern African studies, 11*(1). Today the anthropologist Keith Hart is claimed the coiner of the term "informal economy" in since his pioneering work in Ghana focusing on low-income activities, among workers unable to find legal wage employment, in the capital city

[1] In literature we find an aboundancy of definition of shadow economy. In Smith (1994), for instance, we trace a definition that shadow economy comprised "market-based production of goods and services, whether legal or illegal, that escapes detection in the official estimates of GDP" (Smith, 1994, p. 18). The definitions derived form, e.g., Dell'Anno and Schneider (2004) or Feige (1989), define shadow economy in broad terms arguing that those are all economic activities that are left outside the circumvent government regulation, taxation or observation". More conceptualizations on shadow economy may be traced in influential works of See Frey and Pommerehne (1984), Thomas (1992), Loayza (1996), Lippert and Walker (1997), Bhattacharyya (1999), Schneider (1997, 2005, 2011), Gerxhani (2003), Schneider and Enste (2000, 2002), Schneider and Willams (2013), Alm et al. (2004) and Feld and Schneider (2010).

of Accra we observer steadily growing interest in the field. Next year, in 1972, there was the first ILO World Employment Mission to Kenya. The exhaustive report "*Employment, incomes and equality: a strategy for increasing productive employment in Kenya*" (ILO, 1972) discusses the issues related to informal economy in Kenya, including aspects of education, legal regulations, various employment problems encountered, (un)productivity of male and female labor force, poverty issues and regional biases. Throughout their study they find several unique features of informal labor market. In the ILO (1972) report we read: "*Rather, informal activities are the way of doing things, characterised by—ease of entry, reliance on indigenous resources, family ownership of enterprises, small scale of operation, labour-intensive and adapted technology, skills acquired outside the formal school system and unregulated and competitive markets. Informal-sector activities are largely ignored, rarely supported, often regulated and sometimes actively discouraged by the Government*" (ILO, 1972, p. 6). From Peter M. Gutmann (1985) estimates for U.S. economy made for 1981, we learn that "*subterranean economy at 14–15 per cent of the legal, official economy*" (Gutmann, 1985, p. 19). Gutmann in his pioneering study for U.S. economy observes that the subterranean economy refers to all—not necessary illegal—transactions which are not reported to official statistics, but are done through currency use but also checks and barters. He also label these as "off the books" transactions and payments to the employees. In the same work Gutmann referring to other empirical research regarding shadow economy in U.S. he claims that following various estimates we find that something between 3.5 and 30% of U.S. economic activities remains in the shadow. Probably, that highly differentiated findings regarding the extend of the shadow economy in U.S. in 1980s was the first signal of the problem that all researchers will have to deal with after—massive differences in estimates of the extend of the shadow economy. The issues of defining "the shadow", how to measure it are still in the centre of academic and public debate, while various estimation techniques produce different results. These pioneering studies of the undeclared economy in U.S. have led to several major conclusions like: national production (output) is higher at about 15% than in official books, which leads to the conclusion that both economic growth and living standards are higher than in official statistics, labor productivity is higher as well as inflation, and finally unemployment and poverty are slightly less that in official figures. All the biases mentioned above, in effect, lead to erroneous state policies. Another two pioneering studies regarding parallel economy, but for Europe, are that of J. Skolka—provides an exhaustive empirical evidence for Austria, and that of Weck-Hannemann and B.S. Frey—for Switzerland. Skolka (1985) in his paper summarizes several studies on the shadow economy in Austria. Apart from the estimates of the size of the hidden economy in Austria, which they find to be at approximately 4% total gross domestic product, Skolka writes about various propositions of measuring the undeclared economic activities as well as different causes (like tax losses) and biases in estimates that emergence due to e.g. unstable financial system. Weck-Hannemann and Frey (1985) using various estimation techniques, like inter alia, surveys, discrepancy between various income measures, money and participation approach, as well as structural and causal methods, they find that in mid-1980 the size of the hidden economy in Switzerland is at about 3–4%. Important to say that the study of Weck-Hannemann and Frey (1985) is one of the first initiating discussion on "the best" measures of the size of shadow economy. Micheal O'Higgins presents one of the first papers exploring "The relationship between the formal and hidden economies: an exploratory analysis for four countries" (O'Higgins, 1985). In his study he refers to various authors like, e.g., Feige (1980), Tanzi (1980), Petersen (1982), Matthews (1983) or Cassel (1984)—just to cite few, opening new avenues for international discussion on sizes, measurement methods, causes and consequences of the underground economy.

Starting from these early works due to growing interest on shadow economy authors intended to present various approaches to its definition, identification of its root causes and trials of tracing its size. Despite the fact that according to many scholars the concept of shadow economy remains exceedingly fuzzy which may obscure the analysis and empirical works, today in literature we find a general taxonomy of the underground activities. One of the "traditional" criteria of distinguishing between shadow and non-shadow (reported) economic activities is whether they violate or not established institutional rules of doing business (Feige, 1990). Applying the institutional standard of classification we distinguish four types of underground (shadow) economy: the illegal economy; the unreported economy; the unrecorded economy and the informal economy. First, the illegal economy (the black market) refers to production and distribution of prohibited goods and services, e.g. drug traffics or currency exchanges. Usually, activities falling under illegal economy are lucrative, well-organized international business undermining economic, institutional and legal spheres. Second, the unreported economy refers to those economic activities that evade fiscal rules and tax codes established by national government. In this case the size of the shadow economy is perceived (measured) through the amount of income (usually gained through legal activities) but is not reported to the fiscal system. Therefore the tax gap emerges. This problem of tax evasion is especially substantial in countries that have weak and ineffective tax system and institutional being unable to tackle the problem. Surely, tax evasion engraves budget deficits and causes further weakening of the national economy. Third, the unrecorded economy refers to unrecorded income that if followed established rules should be visible (recorded) in national accounting system. The size of unrecorded economy can measured through the difference between the amount of recorded (visible in national accounts) income and output. The existence of massive unrecorded economy biases various macroeconomic indicators, like e.g. inflation and price level, unemployment rate or national savings. Finally, fourth—the informal economy refers to economic activities that "*circumvent the costs and are excluded from the benefits and rights incorporated in the laws and administrative rules covering property relationships, commercial licensing, labor contracts, torts, financial credit and social security systems*" (Feige, 1990, p. 10). Needless to say that all "forms" of shadow economy are linked among one another and e.g. illegal activities perpetuate tax evasion and so on. In effect the national accounts and economic growth are biases downward, having negative social and economic long-run effects.

Apparently, since the years pioneering works on shadow economy, turbulent times in world economy, including such path-breaking events and economic black swans like collapse of former Soviet Bloc, economies crises in Latin America (in 1980s), Asia (in 1990s) or more recent financial sub-prime-driven crisis that boosted in 2008, along with progressively moving globalization and rapid technological changes that reshaped national and global economies, profoundly contributed to increasingly informalization of labor and markets. Along with the observed massiveness of social, economic and institutional changes and parallelly increasing sizes of unobserved and undeclared work, both theoretical and empirical evidence discussing sizes, measures, causes and consequences started to flourish.

Today, multitude of approaches, definitions, measures and explanations of shadow economy may be traced in academic literature. Professionals have developed a wide bundle of techniques and methodological approaches intending to capture the extend of underground economy and undeclared labor. Available estimates, provided in international reports and in scholarly papers, vary—even if one country is considered, as the results depend on methods applied (e.g. sample surveys, tax audits, currency demand, electricity consumption just to cite few) and quality of raw data used. As found in Schneider and Enste (2000) different methods may produce different results even if given period and country is considered, hence cross-country and in-time comparisons should be made with caution.

Today, when looking at the world map, the magnitude of undeclared labor may seem to be astonishing. The problem is especially sever in poorer and economically backward world regions, suffering from political instability, weak state and ineffective institutions. In ILO (2018) report "Women and men in the informal economy. A statistical picture" we trace evidence of the first global (for more than 100 countries) estimates of informal employment. It reports that 61%[2] of workers globally represent informal labor market, which accounts for something like two billion people worldwide. When the world regions, according to GDP level, are considered, according to ILO estimates in developed, developed and emerging countries the informal employment (as share of total employments) is at around 18%, 90% and 67% respectively. It unveils rather obvious negative association between level of economic development and the size of informal employment. If decomposing data on informal employment by region[3] Sub-Saharan Africa is the "leader" where 89% of total employment accounts for informal labor; then Southern Asia and East and South-East Asia achieving 88% and 77% accordingly. In Middle East and North Africa, Latin America and Caribbean, Eastern Europe and Central Asia, ILO (ILO, 2018) report "only" 68%, 54% and 37% of informal labor respectively. Going into more details, we see that agriculture and services are much more prone to economic informality than manufacturing sector, where "only" 18% of total labor is found as informal.

[2] ILO estimates are based on harmonized definition of informality to micro-data from more than 100 countries (ILO, 2018).

[3] If developed economies are excluded.

Figure 2.1 pictures time trends in informal employment for selected developing countries between 2000 and 2019. Except South Africa where the informal employment rate is reported to be relatively the lowest and shows tendency to drop since 2000 onward, in the remaining countries the size of employment informality remains rather high and stable between 2000 and 2019. Only in some countries slight drops are traceable, while in Honduras a radical shift is reported (from 63.5% in 2006 to 75% in 2017, with the observable peak in 2014 at 89%).

Drawing this global picture in regard to informal employment, in this snapshot there arise several "worst examples" of countries where the estimated informal employment is the highest (WDI, 2020). Among these inglorious economies we trace Congo Dem. Rep. (97% in 2004), Benin (95% in 2011), Burkina Faso (94% in 2018), Burundi (90% in 2014), or Liberia and India (approx. 90% for both countries

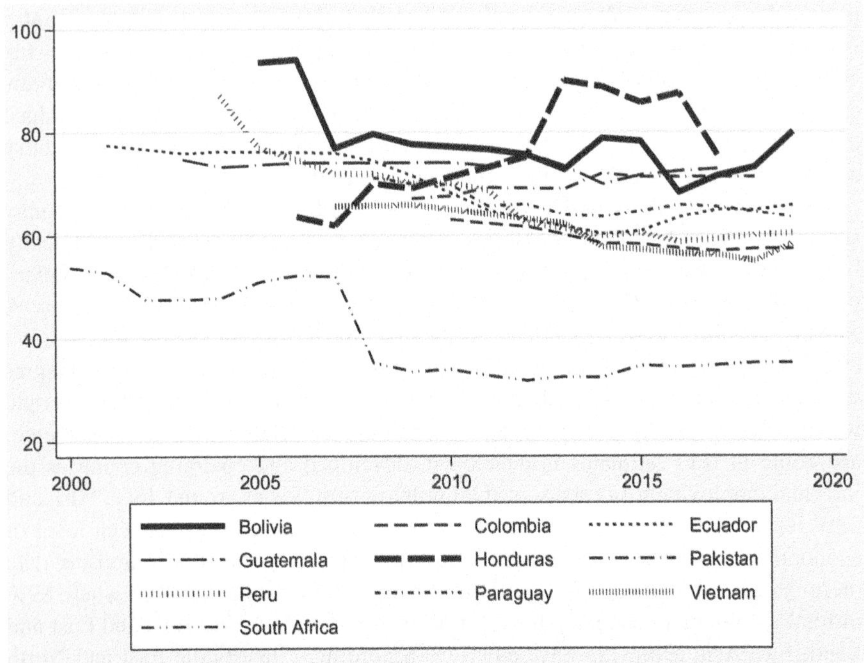

Fig. 2.1 Informal employment (% of total employment). Source: Authors' elaboration based on data derived from World Development Indicators database 2020. Note: Informal employment (Employment in the informal economy as a percentage of total non-agricultural employment. It basically includes all jobs in unregistered and/or small-scale private unincorporated enterprises that produce goods or services meant for sale or barter. Self-employed street vendors, taxi drivers and home-base workers, regardless of size, are all considered enterprises. However, agricultural and related activities, households producing goods exclusively for their own use (e.g. subsistence farming, domestic housework, care work, and employment of paid domestic workers), and volunteer services rendered to the community are excluded (extracted from World Development Indicators database 2020).) in here refers to informal employment as share of total non-agricultural employment

in 2014 and 2018 accordingly) just to cite few. Importantly to note that for all of examples mentioned above, statistics on the size of informal economy are not collected on regular basis, hence this data are highly fragmented and scattered. However, it inevitably leads to the conclusion that in a great majority of Latin American and African economies a huge part of national product is generated but not registered in formal statistics. That suggest the existence of the second parallel, unsanctioned economy to the official one. In countries with massive undeclared economy informal labor plays a significant role in employment and national product creation, and is recognized as an important source of income. Despite these spurious advantages that the existence of extensive unofficial economy can bring to society, notably informal employment puts workers into economic vulnerability as their incomes are instable, prone to external shocks. Indeed, in economically backward countries informal employment is often the only alternative but at the same time it has adverse impact on occupational safety, working and health conditions, offers low-productive and low-paid works.

At the other extreme we find countries where high-income economically developed countries where, on average, approx. 18% of labor falls under informal employment (ILO, 2018). In the research of Medina and Schneider (2018), they use macro and adjusted MIMIC approach to estimate size of shadow economy in European countries. According to their estimates the average size of the shadow economy in 27 examined European countries is between 10 and 16% of domestic production (according to difference methods), while among countries with smallest size of informal economy are Switzerland (4–6%), Austria (4.6–7%), Luxembourg (5.3–8%), Netherlands (5.5–8.4%) and United Kingdom (6–9.4%). At the other extreme we find countries like Bulgaria, Turkey, Croatia, Romania and Estonia for which estimated sizes of shadow economy are at around 20–25% (averaged value of the results from macro and MIMIC methods used) of domestic production.

A wide bundle of problems associated with undeclared labor, income and production differ fundamentally between high-income and developed countries, transition economies, and low-income economically poor countries. These groups of countries substantially differ among one another in terms of causes and consequences of shadow economy, institutional and legal context, gender, age and branch of industry composition regarding informal employment, but also structure of national economy, social norms and attitudes, level of education, urbanization that are not-neutral in this case. Economically backward countries suffer from various deficiencies ranging from poor institutions and shortages in backbone infrastructure, through permanently lacking financing resource to invest and poorly working economy, to inefficient health and educational systems. Widespread material poverty, political conflicts, corruption add to the picture. Co-existence of two types of economies in developing countries, formal and informal ones, seems to natural. By some estimates close to 100% of domestic product is generated in the shadow, which means that the real GDP produced is twice as higher as reported in official numbers. In economically poor countries staying in the shadow is often necessity-driven, is the only alternative to work and generate income for living and thus escaping material poverty. Lack of opportunities to join formal part of economy and labor market is recognized as one of main drivers of extensive shadow economy in developing countries. The other thing is that due to the mostly agricultural nature of many developing countries, a significant share of labor force is classified as contributing family workers which by definition (see WDI, 2020) are considered informal. In backward countries the problem of informal labor touches mostly poorly educated young women, living in rural areas. For instance, in Sub-Saharan Africa 90% of women work in the shadow, compared to men where "only" 82% of them fall under informal employment; 94% of those in informal education they do have any formal education (never attended school); in rural areas 89% of labor stay in the shadow while "only" 76% in urbanized regions. In effect, not only in Africa, but in the remaining developing countries a huge share of labor is unreported, they are self-employed vulnerable workers or unpaid family workers, running low-productive and low-beneficiary business, with neither social nor legal protection, exposed to external risks. However, arguably unreported labor contributes to the overall economy, provides at least minimal (although unstable) source of livelihood and allows to escape extreme material poverty and contributes to gradual elimination of gender inequality in labor market and other economic activities.

The root causes of the shadow economy in relatively rich and developed countries differ substantially from what is observed in the developing and poor parts of the world. It seems that in developed and the so called transition countries[4] undeclared economic activities are closely related, and a direct consequence of extensive tax and social security burdens, as well as intensity of regulations in regard to the tax system itself, but also labor market, trade barriers and other restrictions that enhance increases in the size of shadow economy (Williams & Schneider, 2013). Tax burden, low tax morale enhance directly tax evasion, which in effect lowers budgetary incomes from taxes, and hence in public goods and services delivery (Enste, 2018). Growing budget deficit impedes state infrastructure investments, but also impeded spending on healthcare and educational system, research and development, which—in the long run perspective, reduces economic growth and overall socio-economic welfare. Existence of weak institutions intensifies undeclared economic activities, which—inevitably, leads to further undermining of state institutions being a real treat for economic and political stability. According to Enste (2018) estimations (basing on macroeconomic data) of sizes of shadow economy (as share of gross domestic product) in industrialized countries between 2003 and 2018, we see that the problem of staying in the shadow reveals to be the most significant in transition economies (c) and countries in the south of Europe. As reported, the average for 2003–2018, reaches 34% in Bulgaria, 31.5% in Romania, approx. 30% in Lithuania, Estonia and Turkey; in Latvia, Cyprus, Poland and Greece it exceeds 26% of GDP. On the other extreme we trace four countries where estimated size of the shadow economy in under 10% of GDP, these are: Japan, Austria, Switzerland and the United States. Facing the fact that sizes of shadow economy

[4] The term refers to countries undergoing structural stranformation from centrally-plan to free market economy. In Europe it refers to former Soviet Union and Eastern Block countries, while also some economies from the Third World are now claimed to be transition economies.

seems to be relatively large even in high-developed industrialized countries, governments try to undertake various actions to fight shadow economy, especially to fight illegal business like smuggling or drug traffic. Punitive fines and tight state controls are to a large extend infective way to reduce informality. Apparently country-specific approach in undertaking actions against shadow economy is needed, and adequate policy strategies shall be developed. Probably better and more friendly regulations, more fair and transparent tax system, as well as better governed and stronger institutions would discourage people from accepting unreported jobs and/or income et alia (Huynh, Nguyen, Nguyen, & Nguyen, 2020; Pieth, 2018; Plotnikov, Golovko, Fedotova, & Rukinov, 2019).

2.2 Why People Choose Shadow Economy?

Extensive shadow economy may be claimed as one of the free-market failure, which emergence if enforce by unfriendly legal regulations, extensive tax burden and low tax morale, high labor costs imposed on employers, or simply weak national institutions. Needless to say that the presence of the shadow economy shows that state macroeconomic policies are usually overly burdensome or even oppressive to some point so that people simply prefer escaping formal employment and market activities and go into shadow. Existing economic policies with respect to taxation system or any other that constitute legal framework are claimed to be essential. To some extend examining the size of the shadow economy is also important from a different angle—it allows us understanding how extensive government policy shapes both individuals and enterprises market behavior. Examining the extent of and reasons why shadow economy emerges in given economy is important for many reasons. With regard to given economy the size of the shadow economy may constitute a valuable source of information—mostly for governments, about policy flaws like, inter alia, suboptimal taxation system or other regulations. The presence of an active shadow economy undeniably reflects the degree to which existing economic policies are inappropriate or inefficient. Next, shadow economy activities are basically untaxed and hence they reduce state revenues that potentially might be obtained from corporate income tax. That said that people working in the 'shadow economy' they simply escape taxation and thus state tax revenues are lower than potentially could be if all economic activities would have been registered.

Identifying and understanding major factors that determine the emergence and the size of the shadow economy, remains critical to challenge the problem. It is not only important from the state policy perspective, but is also gives fundamental knowledge on how given economy works and let us learn about it deficiencies in some areas. Examining why people 'remain in the shadow' is also important for economic development strategy designing, as it enables differentiated policies to enhance the reduction of the shadow economy and thus foster economic efficiency and effectiveness. Reasons standing behind the individuals' decision to participate in the shadow economy usually is not exogenously driven, but depends on multiple political, economic, social and institutional factors. Still our knowledge on main drives of the shadow economy is relatively scattered. Following works of, inter alia, Schneider and Williams, we find out that the size of the unregistered work in different countries may be subjected to individual decisions made by labor force, which are determined by legal framework and intensity of regulations, tax morale and tax burden, quality of institutions, labor market regulations and even culture. Needless to say that significance of these factors varies across countries.

Both in conceptual and empirical literature the following causes are traced. In one of the pioneering studies of Allingham and Sandmo (1972) we find claims that the tax evasion (both for direct and indirect taxes) are the major determinant of going into the shadow. In the work of Schneider and Neck (1993) they argue that the income tax system "complexity" stands behind the extensive shadow economy. Using the example of Austrian tax system and considering its modifications on consecutive years (1973, 1984, 1989) they expected that decreases in tax burdens would directly lead to reducing sizes of shadow economy. They found their supposition just partially true, as introduced in 1989 in Austria significant changes in tax structures did not generate radical drops in the size of the shadow economy. Hence, it is not only the tax burden but also the complexity of the whole tax system that affects the shadow economy. Basically, tax system (tax burdens) and social security contribution burdens are widely considered as ones of the major drivers of the shadow economy. Many researchers especially find excessive taxation as an important determinant of the shadow economy. Williams and Schneider argue that "*the bigger the difference between the total labour cost in the official economy and after-tax earnings from work, the greater is the incentive to reduce the tax wedge by working in the shadow economy. Both the levels of social security taxes and the overall tax burden are key determinants of both the existence of and changes in the size of the shadow economy*" (Williams & Schneider, 2013, p. 37–38). The arguments supporting the supposition that this tax and social security contribution burdens heavily impacts the size of the shadow economy may be traced in a wide bundle of studies like, inter alia, in several earlier works of Lippert and Walker (1997), Schneider (1994, 1997, 2005, 2009), Johnson, Kaufmann, and Zoido-Lobaton (1998), Tanzi (1999), Giles (1999), or Eilat and Zinnes (2002) and Davis and Henrekson (2004); but also in the most recent empirical, often country-case based evidence, like reported in Angour and Nmili (2019), Dell'Anno and Davidescu (2019), Pozdnyakova, Bogoviz, Lobova, Ragulina, and Popova (2019), Schneider, Khan, Hamid, and Khan (2019) or Almenar, Sánchez, and Sapena (2020) just to cite few examples.

Another, broadly recognized in literature determinant of the shadow economy are density and intensity of regulations in the official economy, especially on labor markets, trade and doing business spheres. Over-regulations of economy reducing various freedoms, they should lead to radical drops in intensity of registered economic activities. On the other hand, limitating regulations enhance increases of the shadow economic activities. Surely, potential penalties for tax evasion and probability of sanctions are closely related to regulation aspects, and not neutral in case of propensity to flee to the shadow economy. In case of intensive labor market regulations we often face the issues of high labor costs, hence both side of the labor market (employer and employee) wish to avoid them. Needless to say that shadow workers are excluded from the social protection system, may not claim any welfare benefits, stay "outside the labor law" which makes them prone unexpected changes and exposed to external risks. Undeclared workers are often classified as vulnerable workers (Mitrus, 2014) as they are not protected by any e.g. social system and are at permanent risk of losing their job and hence being left without any social protection. In Kelmanson, Kirabaeva, Medina, and Mircheva (2019) recognize several factors closely related to the density and intensity of regulations in the formal economy that effectively enforce informal employment, especially when people experience difficulties in finding formal work. They label it exit factors and list issues discouraging workers from formal employment, and these are: regulatory burden and costly regulation (e.g. high labor costs), complicated and weak tax system, corruption and extensive administrative barriers, weak labor market institution and low quality public services (e.g. social protection), or perceiving higher benefits from being informally than formally employed. In literature we also find traces of the so called exclusion factors (when workers prefer to rely on themselves to provide income subsistence) that enhance people to join shadow economy and work as undeclared labor force. Among these we find again regulatory burden and high labor costs, but also lack of valuable opportunities in the formal economy, low skills and low human capita that disables workers to find well-paid and permanent job. The exclusion factors seem to play a significant role in rural areas where workers usually tend to be less educated with lower skills, and are usually employed in labour-intensive sectors characterized by relatively lower productivity. Moreover, in rural regions a significant share of labor is often recognized as contributing family workers which, by definition, are undeclared worker. Still, in poorer regions such form of employment plays an important role in material poverty eradication and providing safety nets for deprived population.

Finally, scholars claim that weak intuitions, combined with declining tax morale and loyalty towards state institutions and corruption significantly contribute to size of the shadow economy. According to Friedman, Johnson, Kaufmann, and Zoido-Lobaton (2000), Teobaldelli (2011) or Buehn and Schneider (2012) good quality of state institution may effectively diminish the size of the shadow economy. Well-developed efficient and not overcomplicated tax systems seem to be even more important than tax burdens. Workers demonstrate less propensity to flee to underground economy if government institutions and systems work well, are workers-friendly and are little corrupted (Baklouti & Boujelbene, 2020; Berdiev, Goel, & Saunoris, 2018; Gillanders & Parviainen, 2018). Better institutions and sound regulations ensure rule of law, secure property rights and contract enforceability which are quite obvious benefits and incentives to behave legally and to stay in the registered part of the economic system.

The last important element that determines the shadow economy is tax morale (Bruno, 2019; Kemme, Parikh, & Steigner, 2020; Torgler & Schneider, 2009). Song and Yarbrough (1978) write that tax morale are "*the norms of behaviour governing citizens as taxpayers in their relationship with the government*" (Song & Yarbrough,

1978, p. 443). Tax morale can be also linked to taxpayer ethics and may be perceived as moral obligation to pay taxes and in that way contributing to society welfare. The issues associated with tax morale edge with psychological aspects of economic behaviours, social norms and attitudes towards taxes; it regards the question to what extent societies consider their moral duties to pay taxes, which implies that it goes beyond solely regulatory (legal) aspects of taxation systems (Mickiewicz, Rebmann, & Sauka, 2019). Tax morale tackles the problem if societies treat paying taxes as their moral duty, and—consequently, if and when tax evasion would be morally justified (Alm & Torgler, 2006; Larsen, 2019; Molero & Pujol, 2012).

In work of Enste (2018) we find a compilation of data derived from Eurobarometer 2014 explaining main reasons for staying in the undeclared part of the economy in Europe. According to Enste (2018) calculations an important driver of feeing into the shadow is the inability to find a regular job; that reason was declared by 40% of surveyed workers in Southern Europe and almost 30% in East and Central Europe. Approximately 30% of surveyed workers in Southern Europe indicated they stay in the shadow as they have no other means of income; while in East and Central European countries it was just 20%. According to the same survey, both in East and Central Europe and Southern Europe approximately 20% of surveyed workers stated that tax burdens and excessively high social security contributions are the reasons why they chose to work in the shadow. Interestingly in Nordic countries the reason of too high tax burdens was claimed by only 10% of surveyed workers. A surprising conclusion from Enste (2018) calculations is that in Nordic countries and Continental Europe approximately 65% of surveyed persons declared that they decided to work in the shadow as it was beneficial for both sides of the market. Next in the same study of Enste (2018) we find his estimates[5] regarding main factors influencing the shadow economy in industrial countries. Depending on the number of past studies included in his estimations (15 of 28), his unequivocally reports that taxes and social security contributions demonstrate the most significant influence on the shadow economy: 35%–38% and 45%–52% if 15 and 28 of studies were included accordingly. Tax morale was the second significant factor affecting the size of the shadow economy. Another three examined elements: intensity of state regulations, costs of social contributions and labor market regulations he found as of relatively little importance for the shadow economy in industrialized economies.

Today, the empirical evidence on elements driving the shadow economy is abundant. For last years it usually concentrates on specific world regions or is country-based. For instance, in work of Goel and Nelson (2016) they discriminate between developed and developing nations finding that bureaucratic complexity and over-regulation of business sphere enhance workers to flee into shadow. Gasparėnienė, Remeikienė, and Heikkila (2016) present the evidence for Ukraine and they find that almost 99% of Ukrainian shadow economy can be explained by high tax rates;

[5] Estimates based on results reported in Enste, D. H., and F. Schneider. "Zum Spannungsfeld von Politik und Ökonomie." Jahrbuch Schattenwirtschaft, Band 1 and 2. Vienna: Lit Verlag, 2006 and 2011; Schneider, F., and D. H. Enste. The Shadow Economy—An International Survey. 2nd edition. Cambridge, UK: Cambridge University Press, 2013.

they also find that despite the fact of growing possibility of finding legal job, the probability of joining illegal labor market remains high. In different study for Ukraine, that of Bilan, Vasylieva, Lyeonov, and Tiutiunyk (2019), the authors show that investment volume and the shadow economy are inversely related. Berdiev, Pasquesi-Hill, and Saunoris (2015) in their evidence for the United States they find that capital tax rates, educational attainment, union participation affect the size of the shadow economy. Bayar (2016) in his study for Baltic States he finds that corruption and little political freedom drive the shadow economy. In Huynh and Nguyen (2019) evidence for Asian economies where the shadow economy is driven by corruption, expansionary fiscal policies and tax burden. Din, Habibullah, and Hamid (2019) report that in Malaysia lower personal tax rate discourages workers from participating in the shadow economy, while—on the other hand, growing material poverty in some country regions enforces people to stay in the shadow labor market. An interesting evidence is traced in Alarcón-García, Azorín, and de la Vega (2020) in which the authors examine the Hofstede cultural variables versus the shadow economy. Their study strongly confirm that national culture and the state of development of given country heavily determine the size of the shadow economy.

2.2.1 *Determinants of the Shadow Economy in Poland: Past Evidence*

Transition countries in Central and Eastern Europe as well as states of former Soviet Union are economies where economies, social and institutional factors are rather specific, and to a large extent enhance decision to participate in the shadow economy. In early 1990s when the Soviet Block collapsed, newly emerged countries where economically, socially and institutionally devastated, corruption was common and "well-grounded". The existence of overwhelming corruption had multiple negative consequences, like e.g. rising costs of doing business, waste of public resources, further weakening of state and legal structures and trust for the state (Bayar, Odabas, Sasmaz, & Ozturk, 2018). The transformation process, implemented shock therapies, fundamental structural shifts of national economies, hyperinflation and structural unemployment became "perfect" ground for the shadow economy to boost. According to Schneider (2002) estimates in 2000–2001 the average size of the shadow economy[6] (as % of registered GDP) was 66%, 60%, 52%, 45% respectively in Georgia, Azerbaijan, Ukraine and Armenia; while the average for all post-Soviet states was close to 45%. Analogous estimates for Central and Eastern European countries, as an average for 2000–2001, was close to 30% of registered GDP, with the top-shadow economies of Macedonia (45%), Bulgaria (37%) or Romania (34%). Schneider (2002) estimate of the size of the shadow

[6] Using DYMIMIC method.

economy for Poland for 2000–2001 was almost 28% of official GDP, and approximately 20% of labor force was working in the shadow.

In Poland, the shadow economy still remains the area relatively poorly explored, data are not collected on annual basis, while estimates offered by various authors differ significantly. Although Statistics Poland has conducted a survey study on unregistered work since 1995 onward, in terms of scientific research only few scholars tackle this issue. Between 2004 and 2015 analysis regarding main causes of 'staying in the shadow economy' was done by National Statistical Office, for 2015 and 2016 such reports have been completed by the Gdansk Institute for Market Economics, in 2019 two more reports were issued by Polish Economic Institute and Institute for Forecasts and Economic Analysis. Some, although rather fragmented evidence on causes of the shadow economy in Poland evidence in traced in works of Zabrzeska-Bicz (1995), Zienkowski (1996), Szopa (1998), Pilarska (1999), Gołębiowski (2007), Owczarczyk (2007), Kubiczek (2008), Kabaj (2009), Poławski (2009), Cichocki and Tyrowicz (2010), and more recent works of Łapiński, Peterlik, and Wyżnikiewicz (2015), Szarek and Okliński (2016), Fundowicz, Łapiński, Peterlik, and Wyżnikiewicz (2016), Pasternak-Malicka (2019), Malaczewska (2019).

Before 2004 the analysis on the shadow economy in Poland are more scattered and lack consistency to a large extend. Some statistical evidence may be found in, for instance, work of Kabaj (2009) where we find both data and causal analysis of undertaking undeclared job in Poland between 1995 and 2004. He reports that during the period 1995–2004 the total number of people working in the 'shadow d economy' has substantially dropped from 2,199,000 in 1995 until 1,431,000 in 1998, and then in 2004 anther decrease was noted until 1,317,000; henceforth we have observed a significant fall by about 34% during that period. In his work Kabaj (2009) distinguished five major determinants of taking unregistered job. These were following: insufficient income, inability to find job, high taxes, higher pay without contract, high insurance rate; however as he noted between 1995 and 2004 the impact of these five aspects differed significantly (see Table 2.1).

Evidently the most important 'reason' for working in the shadow was insufficient income and in 1995 as 66% of respondents declared it to be the major determinants. On the second place with 42% of responses—still in 1995—we found inability to find job. Interestingly, after 10 years of dynamic transformation of Polish economy, in 2004, 68% of people survey responded that they stay in the shadow due

Table 2.1 Reasons for staying in the shadow economy

Reasons for staying in the shadow economy	1995	1998	2004
Insufficient income (%)	66	59	45
Inability to find job (%)	42	59	68
High taxes (%)	26	24	13
Higher pay without contract (%)	18	22	21
High insurance rate (%)	16	17	22

Poland between 1995 and 2004

Source: Authors' compilation based on data provided in Kabaj (2009)

to inability to find job, while 'only' 45% of them declared insufficient income as an obstacle. These results suggest that until 2004 labor market in Poland was working ineffectively, labor market institutions were working poorly. Moreover, bearing in mind the fact that on average more than 50% of responds declared insufficient income as the major determinant of undertaking job in the shadow, it inevitably leads to the conclusion material deprivation is still a problem in Poland. The latter seems to be of special importance especially if considering the fact that the remaining three factors like high tax, higher pay without tax and high insurance rate, were reported as elements of far less importance.

Figure 2.2 and Table 2.2 summarize the results of the surveys presented in Statistics Poland reports for the years 2004, 2009, 2010, 2014 and 2017, aiming to identify reasons for fleeing into shadow labor market. Statistics in Table 2.2 additionally discriminate between rural and urban regions in Poland, for the years as listed above.

Consecutive Statistics Poland reports on unregistered unemployment in Poland (years 2004, 2009, 2010, 2014 and 2017) using survey method of data collection intend to identify major factor that determine the size of the shadow economy.

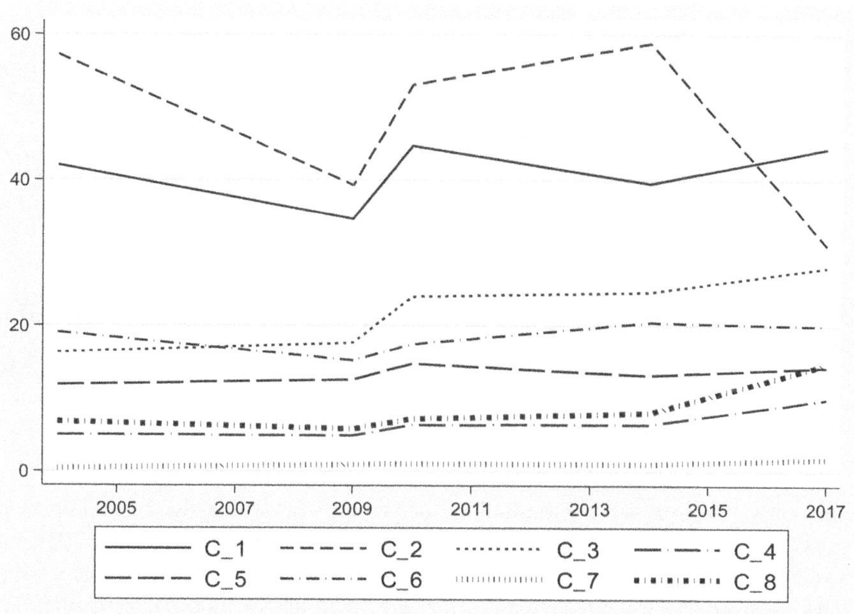

Fig. 2.2 Reasons for 'staying in the shadow'; share of total unregistered workers. Poland, period 2004–2017. Source: Authors' elaborations based data derived from Statistics Poland reports (2004, 2009, 2010, 2014 and 2017). Note: C_1: insufficient income; C_2: inability to find a job; C_3: employer proposes higher pay without formal employment contract; C_4: Family/personal reasons; C_5: taxes discourage from registering income; C_6: high insurance rate; C_7: unwillingness to have a permanent job; C_8: possibility to lose some benefits in case of taking registered work. Outcomes don't sum to 100%, as each surveyed person could choose more than answer from the cafeteria

Table 2.2 Reasons for 'staying in the shadow labor market'

Reasons for staying in the shadow labor market	2004		2009		2010		2014		2017	
	Urban	Rural	Urban	Rural	Urban	Rural	Urban	Rural	Urban	Rural
Total	62.7	37.3	62.0	38.0	61.7	38.3	60.8	39.2	60.1	39.9
Insufficient income	62.6	37.4	61.8	38.2	60.1	39.9	59.4	40.6	60.1	39.9
Inability to find job	62.1	37.9	57.9	42.1	58.5	41.5	58.3	41.7	53.2	46.8
Employer proposes higher pay without formal employment contract	63.7	36.3	65.8	34.2	64.2	35.8	62.6	37.4	61.6	38.4
Family/personal reasons	58.8	41.1	60.1	39.9	62.8	42.0	61.4	38.6	60.0	40.1
Taxes discourage from registering income	66.1	33.9	62.4	37.6	67.6	32.4	62.2	37.8	65.9	34.1
High insurance rate	65.7	34.3	63.6	36.4	63.5	36.5	62.9	37.1	62.9	37.1
Unwillingness to have a permanent job	50.0	49.2	57.2	42.5	68.3	31.7	54.1	45.9	65.8	34.2
Possibility to lose some benefits in case of taking registered work	65.3	34.7	68.1	31.9	67.8	32.2	68.3	31.7	62.3	37.7

Difference between urban-rural areas. Share of total unregistered employment. Poland, period 2004–2017

Source: Authors' compilation based on data derived from Statistics Poland reports (2004, 2009, 2010, 2014 and 2017). Note: outcomes don't sum to 100%, as each surveyed person could choose more than answer from the cafeteria

The study bases on surveys run among of people who are engaged in unreported work, conducted parallel with the Labour Force Survey. Between 2004 and 2014 the results seem to be relatively stable. Among motives for undertaking undeclared work they list three main factors, which are: inability to find a job, insufficient income, and possibility of getting higher pay without formal employment contract. The first element—inability to find a job in 2004 was declared by more than 57% of surveyed workers, and in 2014—by 59%. The insufficient income was reported by approximately 35–45% of surveyed workers between 2004 and 2014; while possibility of getting higher pay without formal employment contract seemed to be an interesting alternative for approximately 20% of surveyed workers. Another two important reasons for undertaking to work in the unreported part of the labor market were excessive tax burdens and high rates of social insurances and that reason was declared by about 11–15% and 15–20% of surveyed workers accordingly. Between 2004 and 2014 unwillingness to have a permanent job and possibility to lose some benefits in case of taking registered work were of minor importance for the shadow economy in Poland. Interestingly, in 2017 we observe noticeable changes in major driving factors of fleeing into shadow labor market. Inability to find a job was the reason of moving into the shadow economy declared by only 31% of surveyed workers, compared to almost 58% in 2014. In 2017 we also observe an increase of the importance of the possibility of getting higher pay without formal employment contract—up to 28%, and excessive taxation—up to 14%. Interestingly the possibility to lose some benefits in case of taking registered work was declared close to 15% of surveyed workers, which results to be the highest score between 2004 and 2017. Surprisingly these opinions do not differ hugely when discriminating between rural and urban regions. Table 2.2 reports the differences between rural and urban areas in regard to determinants of fleeing into shadow labor market. Between 2004 and 2017 we do not observe radical changes in difference between rural and urban regions, expect two elements, namely: inability to find a job and unwillingness to have a permanent job. During the examined period, the inability to find a job as a reason to stay in the shadow economy grew comparably by those living in rural areas compared to those in urban regions; while the reverse trend is observed in case of the unwillingness to have a permanent job. In regard to remaining reasons the structure of answers did not change significantly between rural and urban regions.

Referring again to Statistics Poland reports (2004, 2009, 2010, 2014 and 2017), if differentiating people in terms of their level of education, they declared that the main reason to undertake undeclared job is the inability to find regular job. Apparently, in Poland the main reason that people decide to work in the shadow are closely associated with poor labor market development and are typically economic ones. In fact, in the study the authors did not report institutional determinants and these related to high tax burden or low tax morale. In previous reports of undeclared job in Poland prepared by Statistics Poland, for instance in those from 2009 or 2010, we read that the main reasons of 'staying in the shadow' remain unchanged and are primarily associated with inability to find job in formal sector and low incomes. In work of Cichocki and Tyrowicz (2010) we find more evidence on the reasons why people undertake unregistered work, and to a large extend their results coincide with those presented in annual reports. Cichocki and Tyrowicz confirm that the main reason of working in the shadow is permanent inability to find legal and registered job, and thus working "in the shadow" remains the only possibility to acquire job and ensure source of income. In their study they also report that in Poland seeking job in undeclared sector is rather a necessity that just free choice, caused by poorly developed labor market. Next, the same authors in Cichocki and Tyrowicz (2011) claim during the economic slowdown people demonstrate higher propensity to undertake undeclared job, which is strictly associated with difficulties of finding regular and registered job. Moreover they find that low-skilled labor force undertakes informal jobs more often that high-qualified people. In work of Cichocki (2016) we find repeated evidence causes of undeclared work existence in Poland as that in Cichocki and Tyrowicz (2010, 2011). In work of Nogalski, Karpacz, and Wójcik-Karpacz (2004) we find evidence that workers tend to work as unregistered works mainly due to high social and income taxes, need to compete on the market and high pressure to lower costs of running business. Similar claims have been raised in work of Gołębiowski (2007). In his work he also underlines the unique role of psychological determinants of undertaking informal job, and he argues that these are mainly associated with broadly perceived tax morale and risk aversion.

Looking at the problem of the shadow economy in Poland from the companies and employers perspective the elements that push entrepreneurs to hide in the shadow are obviously different compared to those declared by people seeking for job. According to Fundowicz, Łapiński, Peterlik, and Wyżnikiewicz (2019), one of the main reasons of the significant shadow economy in Poland is excessive tax burden, overregulation of the labor market and doing business, high costs of labor and other costs associated with running a company, high minimum wage which generates high propensity to leave the formal economy and jump into the shadow. Moreover, complex, complicated and often unclear tax system, multiple regulations regarding e.g. technical norms, environment protection, as well as entrepreneurs' attitudes towards the system like low tax morale and high propensity to achieve undeclared and untaxed incomes, also from illegal economic activities.

To show the weakness of the national economy in certain dimensions, potentially by identifying the major causes of the 'shadow economy' emergence may pave road ahead for future economy policy designing. Reducing, that may be achieved only if its root causes are identified, the size of the 'shadow economy' allows increasing the overall effectiveness of the national economy, including effectiveness of the labor market, entrepreneurial sector and—in the longer perspective, both labor and capital productivity. Identifying major causes is important as it allows to elaborate certain ways of escaping the 'shadow economy', despite the fact that estimating the size of shadow (informal) economy still remains a challenging task. Despite multiple attends and tries, still the evidence is mixed, to some point is lack robustness, and to large extend it is predetermined by the measurement techniques applied. Undoubtedly the measurement aspects are the key the in this case.[7] Other difficulties in measuring the shadow economy arise when considering the fact that informal work activities are subjected to, inter alia, legal and especially tax regulations, tax morale, social norms and habits, tax burned and propensity to tax avoidance, the extent of non-wage costs and other multiple labor markets regulations. Another thing is that informal economy activities encompass huge amount of small and geographically dispersed people's activates. All these differ hugely across economies and thus developing a common measure that might be widely adopted is not an easy task.

[7] Scholars use the so called direct procedure to measure shadow economy mostly at micro level, indirect procedures that use a set of macroeconomic indicators to approximate the size of the shadow economy and different statistical tools and models that treat informal economy as unobservable variable.

Despite obviously existing difficulties and limitations, many scholars face the challenge and provide us the evidence on informal economy measures. This evidence, although scattered and fragmented, brings some pieces of knowledge with this respect.

References

Alarcón-García, G., Azorín, J. D. B., & de la Vega, M. D. M. S. (2020). Shadow economy and national culture: A spatial approach. *Hacienda Pública Española, 232*(1), 53–74.

Allingham, M. G., & Sandmo, A. (1972). Income tax evasion: A theoretical analysis. *Journal of Public Economics, 1*(3–4), 323–338.

Alm, J., & Torgler, B. (2006). Culture differences and tax morale in the United States and in Europe. *Journal of Economic Psychology, 27*(2), 224–246.

Alm, J., Martinez-Vazquez, J., & Friedrich, S. (2004). *Sizing the problem of the hard-to-tax*, Working Paper, Georgia State University: USA.

Almenar, V., Sánchez, J. L., & Sapena, J. (2020). Measuring the shadow economy and its drivers: The case of peripheral EMU countries. *Economic Research-Ekonomska Istraživanja, 33*(1), 2904–2918.

Angour, N., & Nmili, M. (2019). Estimating shadow economy and tax evasion: Evidence from Morocco. *International Journal of Economics and Finance, 11*(5), 1–7.

Baklouti, N., & Boujelbene, Y. (2020). Shadow economy, corruption, and economic growth: An empirical analysis. *The Review of Black Political Economy, 47*(3), 276–294.

Bayar, Y. (2016). Public governance and shadow economy in Central and Eastern European countries. *Revista Administratie si Management Public (RAMP), 27*, 62–73.

Bayar, Y., Odabas, H., Sasmaz, M. U., & Ozturk, O. F. (2018). Corruption and shadow economy in transition economies of European Union countries: A panel cointegration and causality analysis. *Economic research-Ekonomska istraživanja, 31*(1), 1940–1952.

Berdiev, A. N., Goel, R. K., & Saunoris, J. W. (2018). Corruption and the shadow economy: One-way or two-way street? *The World Economy, 41*(11), 3221–3241.

Berdiev, A. N., Pasquesi-Hill, C., & Saunoris, J. W. (2015). Exploring the dynamics of the shadow economy across US states. *Applied Economics, 47*(56), 6136–6147.

Bhattacharyya, D. K. (1999). On the economic rationale of estimating the hidden economy. *Economic Journal, 109*, 348–359.

Bilan, Y., Vasylieva, T., Lyeonov, S., & Tiutiunyk, I. (2019). Shadow economy and its impact on demand at the investment market of the country. *Entrepreneurial Business and Economics Review, 7*(2), 27–43.

Bruno, R. L. (2019). Tax enforcement, tax compliance and tax morale in transition economies: A theoretical model. *European Journal of Political Economy, 56*, 193–211.

Buehn, A., & Schneider, F. (2012). Corruption and the shadow economy: Like oil and vinegar, like water and fire? *International Tax and Public Finance, 19*(1), 172–194.

Cassel, D. (1984). The growing shadow economy: Implications for stabilization policy. *Intereconomics, 19*(5), 219–225.

Chen, M., & Carré, F. (2020). *The informal economy revisited: Examining the past, envisioning the future* (p. 326). Taylor & Francis.

Cichocki, S. (2016). Informal work in a post-transition country: Some evidence for Poland. *Prakseologia, 158*(1), 255.

Cichocki, S., & Tyrowicz, J. (2010). Źródła zatrudnienia nierejestrowanego w Polsce. *Bank i Kredyt, 41*(1), 81–98.

Cichocki, S., & Tyrowicz, J. (2011). Determinanty zatrudnienia nierejestrowanego w Polsce w okresach wysokiej i niskiej koniunktury gospodarczej. *Gospodarka Narodowa, 3*(235).

Davis, S. J., & Henrekson, M. (2004). *Tax effects on work activity, industry mix and shadow economy size: Evidence from rich-country comparisons* (No. w10509). National Bureau of Economic Research.

Dell'Anno, R., & Davidescu, A. A. (2019). Estimating shadow economy and tax evasion in Romania. A comparison by different estimation approaches. *Economic Analysis and Policy, 63*, 130–149.

Dell'Anno, R., & Schneider, F. (2004). *The shadow economy of Italy and other OECD countries: What do we know?* Discussion paper. Linz, Austria: Department of Economics, University of Linz.

Din, B. H., Habibullah, M. S., & Hamid, B. A. (2019). Re-estimation and modelling shadow economy in Malaysia: Does financial development mitigate shadow economy? *International Journal of Business & Society, 20*(3), 1062–1075.

Eilat, Y., & Zinnes, C. (2002). The shadow economy in transition countries: Friend or foe? A policy perspective. *World Development, 30*(7), 1233–1254.

Enste, D. H. (2018). The shadow economy in industrial countries. *IZA World of Labor, 2018*, 127. https://doi.org/10.15185/izawol.127.v2

Feige, E. L. (1980). *A new perspective on macroeconomic phenomena: The theory and measurement of the unobserved sector of the United States economy: Causes, consequences and implications*.

Feige, E. L. (Ed.). (1989). *The underground economies. Tax evasion and information distortion*. Cambridge: Cambridge University Press.

Feige, E. L. (1990). Defining and estimating underground and informal economies: The new institutional economics approach. *World Development, 18*(7), 989–1002.

Feld, L. P., & Schneider, F. (2010). Survey on the shadow economy and undeclared earnings in OECD countries. *German Economic Review, 11*(2), 109–149.

Frey, B. S., & Pommerehne, W. (1984). The hidden economy: State and prospect for measurement. *Review of Income and Wealth, 30*(1), 1–23.

Friedman, E., Johnson, S., Kaufmann, D., & Zoido-Lobaton, P. (2000). Dodging the grabbing hand: The determinants of unofficial activity in 69 countries. *Journal of Public Economics, 76*(3), 459–493.

Fundowicz, J., Łapiński, K., Peterlik, M., & Wyżnikiewicz, B. (2016). *Szara strefa w polskiej gospodarce w 2016 roku* (p. 7). Warszawa: Instytut Badań nad Gospodarką Rynkową.

Fundowicz, J., Łapiński, K., Peterlik, M., & Wyżnikiewicz, B. (2019). *Szara strefa 2019*. Warsaw: Instytut Prognoz i Analiz Gospodarczych / Institute for Forecasts and Economic Analysis.

Gasparėnienė, L., Remeikienė, R., & Heikkila, M. (2016). Evaluation of the impact of shadow economy determinants: Ukrainian case. *Intellectual Economics, 10*(2), 108–113.

Gerxhani, K. (2003). The informal sector in developed and less-developed countries: A literature survey. *Public Choice, 114*(3–4), 295–318.

Giles, D. E. (1999). Modelling the hidden economy and the tax-gap in New Zealand. *Empirical Economics, 24*(4), 621–640.

Gillanders, R., & Parviainen, S. (2018). Corruption and the shadow economy at the regional level. *Review of Development Economics, 22*(4), 1729–1743.

Goel, R. K., & Nelson, M. A. (2016). Shining a light on the shadows: Identifying robust determinants of the shadow economy. *Economic Modelling, 58*, 351–364.

Gołębiowski, G. (2007). Zjawisko szarej strefy z uwzględnieniem gospodarki polskiej. *Współczesna Ekonomia, 1*(1), 17–28.

Gutmann, P. M. (1985). The subterranean economy, redux. In *The economics of the shadow economy* (pp. 2–18). Berlin: Springer.

Hart, K. (1973). Informal income opportunities and urban employment in Ghana. *The Journal of Modern African Studies, 11*(1), 61–89.

Huynh, C. M., & Nguyen, T. L. (2019). Fiscal policy and shadow economy in Asian developing countries: Does corruption matter? *Empirical Economics*, 1–17.

Huynh, C. M., Nguyen, V. H. T., Nguyen, H. B., & Nguyen, P. C. (2020). One-way effect or multiple-way causality: Foreign direct investment, institutional quality and shadow economy? *International Economics and Economic Policy, 17*(1), 219–239.

ILO. (2018). *Women and men in the informal economy. A statistical picture*. Geneva: ILO.

International Labour Office. (1972). *Employment, incomes and equality: A strategy for increasing productive employment in Kenya*. Geneva: International Labour Office.

Johnson, S., Kaufmann, D., & Zoido-Lobaton, P. (1998). Regulatory discretion and the unofficial economy. *The American Economic Review, 88*(2), 387–392.

Kabaj, M. (2009). Praca nierejestrowana we współczesnej literaturze ekonomicznej. *Polityka Społeczna, 10*, 3–10.

Kelmanson, B., Kirabaeva, K., Medina, L., & Mircheva, B. (2019). *Explaining the shadow economy in Europe: Size, causes and policy options* (IMF Working Paper, WP/19/278, Nov. 2019).

Kemme, D. M., Parikh, B., & Steigner, T. (2020). Tax morale and international tax evasion. *Journal of World Business, 55*(3), 101052.

Kubiczek, A. (2008). Czy szara strefa w Polsce musi być tak rozległa? *Ekonomia i Prawo, 4*, 301–313.

Łapiński, K., Peterlik, M., & Wyżnikiewicz, B. (2015). *Szara strefa w polskiej gospodarce w 2015 roku*. Warszawa: IbnGR.

Larsen, L. B. (2019). What tax morale? A moral anthropological stance on a failed cooperative compliance initiative. *Journal of Tax Administration, 5*(1), 26–40.

Lippert, O., & Walker, M. (Eds.). (1997). *The underground economy: Global evidences of its size and impact*. Vancouver, BC: The Frazer Institute.

Loayza, N. V. (1996). The economics of the informal sector: A simple model and some empirical evidence from Latin America. *Carnegie-Rochester Conference Series on Public Policy, 45*, 129–162.

Malaczewska, P. (2019). *Szara strefa gospodarki. Determinanty i mechanizmy kształtowania*. Wydawnictwo Uniwersytetu Łódzkiego.

Matthews, K. (1983). National income and the black economy. *Economic Affairs, 3*(4), 261–267.

Medina, L., & Schneider, F. (2018). *Shadow economies around the world: What did we learn over the last 20 years?* (IMF Working Paper WP/18/17).

Mickiewicz, T., Rebmann, A., & Sauka, A. (2019). To pay or not to pay? Business owners' tax morale: Testing a neo-institutional framework in a transition environment. *Journal of Business Ethics, 157*(1), 75–93.

Mitrus, L. (2014). The fight against undeclared work: Sanctions and incentives. *European Labour Law Journal, 5*(2), 174–186.

Molero, J. C., & Pujol, F. (2012). Walking inside the potential tax evader's mind: Tax morale does matter. *Journal of Business Ethics, 105*(2), 151–162.

Nogalski, B., Karpacz, J., & Wójcik-Karpacz, A. (2004). Małe przedsiębiorstwa w obliczu gospodarczego cienia, w. In J. Ostaszewski (Ed.), *Polski przedsiębiorca we współczesnym otoczeniu prawno-ekonomicznym*. Warszawa: Oficyna Wydawnicza SGH.

O'Higgins, M. (1985). The relationship between the formal and hidden economies: An exploratory analysis for four countries. In *The economics of the shadow economy* (pp. 127–143). Berlin: Springer.

Owczarczyk, A. (2007). *Gospodarka nieformalna w Polsce* (pp. 379–386). Prace Naukowe/ Akademia Ekonomiczna w Katowicach.

Pasternak-Malicka, M. (2019). Szara strefa–definicje, przyczyny, szacunki. Polska perspektywa zjawiska. *Studia BAS, 2*, 29–56.

Petersen, H. G. (1982). Size of the public sector, economic growth and the informal economy: Development trends in the Federal Republic of Germany. *Review of Income and Wealth, 28*(2), 191–215.

Pieth, M. (2018). Overcoming the shadow economy. *Zeitschrift für die gesamte Strafrechtswissenschaft, 129*(4), 1053–1062.

Pilarska, C. (1999). Gospodarka nieformalna w Polsce ze szczególnym uwzględnieniem szarej strefy rynku pracy. *Zeszyty Naukowe/Akademia Ekonomiczna w Krakowie, 537*, 81–93.
Plotnikov, V., Golovko, M., Fedotova, G., & Rukinov, M. (2019). Ensuring national economic security through institutional regulation of the shadow economy. In *Institute of Scientific Communications Conference* (pp. 342–351). Cham: Springer.
Poławski, P. (2009). Życie na szaro. Wewnętrzne zróżnicowanie szarej strefy. *Polityka Społeczna, 10*, 34–37.
Pozdnyakova, U. A., Bogoviz, A. V., Lobova, S. V., Ragulina, J. V., & Popova, E. V. (2019). The model of well-balanced taxation for overcoming the shadow economy in modern Russia. In *Optimization of the taxation system: Preconditions, tendencies and perspectives* (pp. 207–215). Cham: Springer.
Schneider, F. (1994). Can the shadow economy be reduced through major tax reforms? An empirical investigation for Austria. *Public Finance= Finances publiques, 49*(Suppl), 137–152.
Schneider, F. (1997). The shadow economies of Western Europe. *Journal of the Institute of Economic Affairs, 17*(3), 42–48.
Schneider, F. G. (2002). *The size and development of the shadow economies of 22 transition and 21 OECD countries* (IZA Discussion Papers, No. 514). Bonn: Institute for the Study of Labor (IZA).
Schneider, F. (2005). Shadow economies around the world: What do we really know? *European Journal of Political Economy, 21*(4), 598–642.
Schneider, F. (2009). Size and development of the shadow economy in Germany, Austria and other OECD-countries. *Revue économique, 60*(5), 1079–1116.
Schneider, F. (Ed.). (2011). *Handbook on the shadow economy*. Cheltenham: Edward Elgar.
Schneider, F., & Enste, D. (2000). Shadow economies: Size, causes, and consequences. *The Journal of Economic Literature, 38*(1), 77–114.
Schneider, F., & Enste, D. (2002). *The shadow economy: Theoretical approaches, empirical studies, and political implications*. Cambridge, UK: Cambridge University Press.
Schneider, F., Khan, S., Hamid, B. A., & Khan, A. (2019). *Does the tax undermine the effect of remittances on shadow economy*? (Economics Discussion Papers, No 2019-67). Kiel Institute for the World Economy. Received October 20, from http://www.economics-ejournal.org/economics/discussionpapers/2019-67
Schneider, F., & Neck, R. (1993). The development of the shadow economy under changing tax systems and structures: Some theoretical and empirical results for Austria. *FinanzArchiv/Public Finance Analysis*, 344–369.
Schneider, F., & Willams, C. C. (2013). *The shadow economy*. London: IEA.
Skolka, J. (1985). The parallel economy in Austria. In *The economics of the shadow economy* (pp. 60–75). Berlin: Springer.
Smith, P. (1994). Assessing the size of the underground economy: The Canadian statistical perspectives. *Canadian Economic Observer, 11*, 16–33.
Song, Y. D., & Yarbrough, T. E. (1978). Tax ethics and taxpayer attitudes: A survey. *Public Administration Review*, 442–452.
Szarek, S., & Okliński, D. (2016). Czynniki wpływające na akceptację szarej strefy w społeczeństwie. *Zeszyty Naukowe UPH seria Administracja i Zarządzanie, 36*(109), 87–103.
Szopa, B. (1998). Szara strefa-rynek pracy-poziom życia. *Zeszyty Naukowe/Akademia Ekonomiczna w Krakowie, 515*, 89–103.
Tanzi, V. (1980). The underground economy in the United States: Estimates and implications. *PSL Quarterly Review, 33*(135).
Tanzi, V. (1999). Uses and abuses of estimates of the underground economy. *The Economic Journal, 109*(456), F338–F347.
Teobaldelli, D. (2011). Federalism and the shadow economy. *Public Choice, 146*(3–4), 269–289.
Thomas, J. J. (1992). *Informal economic activity, LSE, handbooks in economics*. London: Harvester Wheatsheaf.

Torgler, B., & Schneider, F. (2009). The impact of tax morale and institutional quality on the shadow economy. *Journal of Economic Psychology, 30*(2), 228–245.

WDI. (2020). *World development indicators database*. World Bank. Retrieved October, 2020, from https://data.worldbank.org/indicator

Weck-Hannemann, H., & Frey, B. S. (1985). Measuring the shadow economy: The case of Switzerland. In *The economics of the shadow economy* (pp. 76–104). Berlin: Springer.

Williams, C. C., & Schneider, F. (2013). *The shadow economy*. London: Institute of Economic Affairs.

Zabrzeska-Bicz, L. (1995). Gospodarka drugiego obiegu a transformacja systemowa w Polsce. *Zeszyty Naukowe/Akademia Ekonomiczna w Krakowie, 450*, 63–73.

Zienkowski, L. (1996). Szacunek rozmiarów szarej strefy [w:] Szara gospodarka w Polsce (rozmiary, przyczyny, konsekwencje). *Studia i Prace Zakładu Badań Statystyczno-Ekonomicznych GUS i PAN*, (233).

Chapter 3
How Large Is Shadow Economy?

Abstract In this chapter we describe the existing methods of measuring shadow economy. We follow the main division defined in the literature, and thus present the measurement methods divided into direct and indirect ones. We recall the most important assumptions related to discussed methods, as well as we point out their major advantages and weaknesses. In this way we locate our approach based on the survey study conducted among companies within another available estimates. This will enable the comparison of obtained results with the previous evidence on the extent of the shadow economy. We also report the existing data on the shadow economy in Poland, provided both by the Statistics Poland as well as another independent research institutes.

3.1 How Large Is Shadow Economy? Methods to Estimate the Size of the Shadow Economy

The exact measurement of the shadow economy and all informal activities conducted both in the registered, unregistered and illegal part of the economy is not possible. The heterogeneous nature of workers performing informal activities results in the need for diversification of the measurement methods. In other words, different methods are dedicated to the analysis of the fragmented parts of the total shadow economy. On the other hand, more important may be even the knowledge on the particular elements of the shadow economy, and indication of its causes, rather than purely calculation of its size (Gérxhani, 2007). In this section we provide an overview of the existing shadow economy measurement methods and report the statistical evidence of the extent of this phenomena.

As the shadow economy is diversified itself, the measurement methods are of different type. As Gérxhani (2007) argue, the choice of method should be related to the aim of the analysis conducted. The most popular division of existing methods is based on the distinction between direct and indirect ones, what is presented in Table 3.1.

In the next sections the most popular direct and indirect methods of measuring shadow economy are presented.

D. Nikulin, E. Lechman, *Shadow Economy in Poland*, SpringerBriefs in Economics, https://doi.org/10.1007/978-3-030-70524-4_3

Table 3.1 Direct and indirect estimation methods of the shadow economy

Indirect methods	Direct methods
Discrepancy between national expenditure and income statistics	Surveys
Discrepancy between the official and actual labor force	Tax /fiscal auditing
Transactions approach	
Currency demand approach	
Electricity consumption method	
MIMIC approach	

Source: Authors' compilation based on Schneider and Buehn (2017)

3.1.1 Indirect Methods in Measuring Shadow Economy

The indirect approach in measuring the extent of shadow economy may be manifolds. The discrepancy methods are based on the differences in the national accounts or the labour market statistics. In particular, one of the way is to use the discrepancies between income and expenditure statistics, namely the income and the expenditure side of the Gross National Product (GNP). Then, the shadow economy proportion may be calculated as the difference between the expenditure and the income measure of GNP. However, this method contains some biases. The biggest weakness in this approach is related to the measurement errors in the national accounts, so the discrepancy contains not only the shadow size of the economy, but also the measurement errors of GNP (Schneider & Buehn, 2017). Among the empirical studies using the national accounts discrepancy method one may mention the estimates from Feld and Larsen (2009) for Germany or from Zukauskas and Schneider (2016) for Baltic states, Poland and Sweden.

Another indirect methods are based on the labor market statistics and the use a difference between the total labor force participation and the official rate as a proxy for shadow economy extent. The study conducted by Nikulin and Sobiechowska-Ziegert (2018) for Poland reveals that the ratio of the number of informally employed (defined as those formally unemployed and at the same time performing informal work) to the total number of employees varies between 0.5 and 1.7% across regions. Naturally, this approach shows some weaknesses. There are people performing hybrid forms of informal employment, with formal main job and additional informal one or people conducting a purely informal job without registration as unemployed. Unfortunately, these groups in the labor market are hard to identify using this approach.

Going further, the transaction method proposed in the nineties by Feige (1996), is based on the Fisher quantity equation $M * V = p * T$ (where M—money, V—velocity, p—prices, and T—transactions). Assuming that the total GNP consists of their official and unofficial part, and expressing the total nominal GNP as the amount of total transactions, the shadow economy, may be derived as a difference between the total nominal GNP and official GNP. However, the theoretical assumptions of this method are perceived as attractive, the empirical verification may be complicated, due to the difficulties related to the necessary statistical data.

The currency demand approach, in turn, developed since the 1950s, firstly by Cagan (1958), then by Gutmann (1977) and Tanzi (1980). The main assumption of this method is to track the demand for currency, which is dictated by the fact that the payments in the shadow part of the economy are predominantly in cash. Obviously the indication is that the higher the extent of the shadow economy, the bigger the demand for currency. Despite the fact, that this method has been applied in many countries, the main limitation is related to the fact, that not all transactions are in cash, moreover most studies take into account only the tax burden as a reason for the shadow economy, while more determinants like impact from the regulations, tax payers' attitudes or tax morality should be considered (Schneider & Buehn, 2017).

In the electricity consumption method (physical input) the main assumption is that the economic activities may be quantified by the electric power consumption. In the approach proposed by Kaliberda and Kaufmann (1996) the electricity consumption may serve as a good indicator for the total domestic product, both their official and unofficial part. In this way, the rise in the electricity consumption is related to the growth in the total Gross Domestic Product. In other words, the elasticity between the electricity and GDP is close to one, what has been empirically proved. The core of this method is therefore very simple: the shadow economy may be calculated as a difference between the electricity consumption and the estimates of official GDP. The main limitations of this method are related to the fact, that some business activities which do not require a substantial amount of electricity may be not indicated, like e.g. personal services. Moreover, due to the technical progress, the efficiency of electricity has been risen over the several decades. Additionally, as significant country heterogeneity in electricity demand is observed (Schneider & Buehn, 2017).

The method proposed by the Lackó (1999), in turn, relates the shadow economy extent with the households consumption of electricity. In this way, using this approach a part of the shadow activities may be estimated including household production, do-it-yourself activities and undeclared production and services. Going further, Laćko assumes that the extent of shadow activities conducted by households are highly correlated to the total size of the shadow economy. The weaknesses of this approach are a bit similar to those of Kaliberda and Kaufmann (1996) one as not all of the shadow activities require so much electricity and moreover, the shadow economy exists beside the households too, what significantly limits the scope of this analysis.

Last, but not least, the Multiple Indicators and Multiple Causes (MIMIC) approach may be applied to measure the extent of the shadow economy. This method, unlike the previous ones, considers many possible causes and multiple indicators to measure the shadow economy. The main assumption here is that the shadow economy is not a purely observable phenomenon and may not be approximated using one indicator. The extent of the shadow economy is therefore quantified by using several causes like the tax and regulations severity and indicators like the amount of cash or the official working hours (Schneider, 2019). Recently, a modified approach proposed by Dybka et al. (2019) proposes a new identification scheme for the MIMIC model in order to address the misspecification issues in the currency demand analysis equations and the vague transformation of the latent variable.

Summing up, the main disadvantage of the indirect methods is their lack of specific information about the informal activities (Gérxhani, 2007), so to gain knowledge about the typical characteristics of those doing informal jobs, the direct methods have to be applied.

3.1.2 Direct Methods in Measuring Shadow Economy

Direct methods are based either on the survey or tax auditing data. These methods provide a good source of gathering data on the nature and characteristics of people and firms engaged in the shadow activities. That's why, the direct methods are mostly used, if the aim of the research is predominantly related not only to the estimation of the size of the shadow economy but also to analyze its causes and structure. However, the sources of the direct methods based on surveys suffer from two major limitations: one is biased estimates due to respondents' untruthful answers and their general reluctance (refusal) to answer sensitive questions or participate in surveys (Groves, 2006); the second is the small size of the samples used (European Commission, 2020). International surveys such as the European Working Conditions Survey, European Social Survey and the recent international labor force survey of undeclared work in the European Union (as a special Eurobarometer survey in 2007, 2013 and 2019) provide cross-country evidence on the prevalence of informal activities across European countries. The remaining evidence is based on national surveys using proxies for informal employment (see among others Di Caro and Nicotra (2016) for Italy, Lehmann (2015) for Russia, Meriküll and Staehr (2010) for the Baltic countries), which simply precludes international comparison.

On the other hand, the drawbacks of the survey studies may be addressed by using tax auditing data. Although the fiscal auditing programs seem to be effective, the main bias is related to the lack of representativeness of audited taxpayers which results in a fragmented picture of the whole shadow economy. This issue was tackled by Beręsewicz and Nikulin (2019) where authors applied a generalization of Heckman's sample selection model, assuming a non-Gaussian correlation of errors and accounting for clustering by incorporation of random effects to correct non-ignorable selection mechanism, to obtain reliable estimates of informal employment in Poland. Since the tax administration scheme is country-specific, other existing (scarce) studies in this field are focused on selected countries, see Di Porto (2011) for Italy or Kriz et al. (2008) for Estonia.

The selected results of the shadow economy surveys will be presented in the Sect. 3.2.

3.2 What Have We Learn So Far? Review of World-Wide Evidence

As indicated in the previous section, the shadow economy measurement methods are of very diversified character what results in the wide range of the estimates of the shadow economy extent. Nowadays, a growing importance of the shadow economy and informal activities not only in developing countries but also in developed ones is underlined (Arendt, Grabowski, & Kukulak-Dolata, 2020). As in developing countries the forms of informal activities are rather simple and include purely informal and unregistered small scale businesses, in developed countries, in turn, the forms of shadow activities are heterogeneous (Heyes & Hastings, 2017) and more challenging to analyze. The problem of undeclared work and related phenomena is of interest to scholars, policy makers and international institutions what is reflected in different international initiatives (e.g. the European Platform tackling undeclared work or WIEGO: Women in Informal Employment: Globalizing and Organizing). In this section we recall the newest available data about the shadow economy extent, using diversified set of measurement methods.

The most prominent and extensive research on measuring shadow economy size is demonstrated in works from F. Schneider. According to his estimates based on the MIMIC model, the size of shadow economy effectively differs across countries, and at very general level it is preconditioned be country's economic welfare. For instance, in rich Anglo-Saxon countries the size of the shadow economy in 2016 varies from 5 to 10% of Gross National Product (USA 5.6%, New Zealand 7.8%,United Kingdom 9.0%, Australia 9.8%), while in relatively poorer Southern European and Eastern European countries it may rise even up to 30% (Bulgaria 30.2%, Romania 27.6%, Croatia 27.1%) (Schneider, 2016). Arguably in economically backward and materially deprived countries the size of shadow economy is much higher. According to Schneider and Williams (2013) in some developing countries the size of shadow economy achieves even 60–70% of GDP and is especially high in agricultural sector where various economic activities are simply never registered. According to different United Nations sources in some poor and underdeveloped economies informal activities may constitute even more than 100% of the formal country's GDP. Schneider most commonly uses the MIMIC method combined with the currency demand method to estimates the size of the shadow economy. His estimates for various economies and years shed light on both size of the shadow economy across examined countries as well as its essential determinants. Figure 3.1 presents the share of shadow economies in GDP in selected European countries in the time period 2003–2016. Interestingly, in all examined economies, from 2003 onward the size of the shadow economy is dropping. The extent of shadow activities in Poland exceeds the level of those activities in other presented countries. There is a significant difference in shadow economy share in Poland in comparison to Austria (23% vs. 7.8% of GDP in 2016), Scandinavian countries like Denmark, Finland and Sweden (11.6%, 12%, 12.6% respectively), but also Central and East Europe Countries like Czech Republic (14.9%).

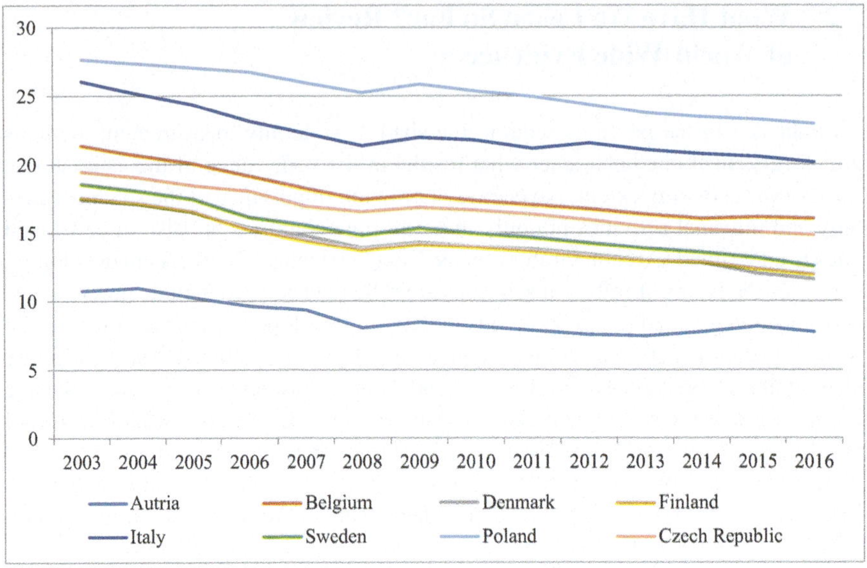

Source: Authors` elaboration based on Schneider (2016).

Fig. 3.1 The share of shadow economy in GDP in selected European countries. Source: Authors' elaboration based on Schneider (2016)

In other research of Schneider, Buehn, and Montenegro (2010) attractive estimates of the shadow economy for different world regions covering country-wise estimates for 162 world countries between 1997 and 2007 are to find. Not surprisingly, the lowest size of the shadow economy is reported in OECD countries; while the highest in 116 developing countries and 25 the so called transition economies. In these two country groups the size of the shadow economy in 1997 was 30% and almost 38% in developing and transition economies respectively; while in 2007 it dropped until 26% and 34%, and hence still was indecently high compared to OECD economies. In the same study we find estimates of the average (for 1997–2007 weighted by GDP of 2005) size of shadow economy in respective geographical world regions, and this research demonstrates that the highest values are for Sub-Saharan Africa (more than 37%), Europe and Central Asia (36.4%) and Latin America and Caribbean (34.7%),while the lowest – high-income OECD economies (13.4%) and East Asia and Pacific (17.5%). The average for the world is calculated for 17.1%.

More evidence on the size of shadow economy for various countries may be also traced in works of, *inter alia*, Schneider and Enste (2013), which constitutes an extensive work on both size and causes of the existence of the informal economy across world countries. Additionally we find more research in Schneider (2015) that demonstrates the results of estimates of the shadow economy for 36 countries between 2003 and 2013. In this study we find data showing that between 2003 and 2013 a significant decline is noted—from 22.3% (averaged values) until 18.5% in

European economies, while in another five non-European countries (Australia, Canada, Japan, New Zealand and the USA) we observe changes in similar direction. Additionally comprehensive research on shadow economy is reported in works of Schneider and Enste (2000), Schneider, Buehn, and Schneider (2007), and Buehn and Schneider (2012).

Despite the huge popularity and prevalence of the MIMIC method, it is not free from weaknesses. The authors are aware, for example, of the problem of double counting while using the macro approach (Feld & Schneider, 2017). Macro MIMIC estimates lead to high values, and therefore to solve partially the problem of double counting a correction (adjustment) is suggested. Table 3.2 contains a cross-country comparison of available data on shadow economy including the adjusted MIMIC estimates. To show the differences in particular calculations we present the estimates for Poland on the background of other European countries. Please note, that we present older MIMIC estimates in order to enable the comparison to other available estimates from this time period. However, the shares of shadow economy in analyzed countries show rather stable level (in the parentheses we recall the newest data related to the year 2016). First of all, a considerable differences between the MIMIC estimates and the adjusted macro estimates may be observed. In case of Poland the difference amounts to almost 9 p.p. (24.7% vs. 16% of GDP in the years 2011–2012), in Czech Republic 5.7 p.p., in Slovak Republic 5.5 p.p. Somewhat

Table 3.2 Size of the shadow economy according to different sources

	Method and reference year	Poland	Czech Republic	Slovak Republic	Austria	Netherlands
Macro estimates	Schneider (macro-MIMIC) 2011–2012	24.7 (23.0)	16.2 (14.9)	15.7 (13.7)	7.6 (7.8)	9.6 (8.8)
	Schneider (adjusted corrected MIMIC) 2011–2012	16	10.5	10.2	4.9	6.2
	National Accounts estimates of NOE (OECD) 2011–2012	15.4	8.1	15.6	7.5	2.3
Micro estimates	Eurobarometer 2013: Envelope wages	5%	5%	7%	2%	3%
	Eurobarometer 2013: Share of employed without formal written contract	2%	0%	0%	2%	1%
	Enterprise survey 2013: Firms competing against unregistered or informal firms	29.1%	36%	42.8%	–	–
	Enterprise survey 2013: Firms identifying practices of competitors in the informal sector as a major constraint	15.3%	23.3%	14.6%	–	–

Source: Authors' compilation based on (European Commission, 2014; Gyomai & van de Ven, 2014; Schneider, 2016, 2017), World Bank database

closer are the results for Austria and Netherlands. Secondly, the results obtained with the use of MIMIC method are considerably higher that the calculations achieved with the National Accounts Discrepancy method for Non-Observed Economy (NOE). The estimates of NOE delivered by the Organization for Economic Cooperation and Development (OECD) are based on national accounts compilation. The data are sourced from the OECD surveys conducted in 2011–2012 and are based the discrepancy method performed at disaggregated level. The national accounts estimates of the NOE cover five major areas: underground production, illegal production, informal sector production, production of households for own-final use and statistical underground (Gyomai & van de Ven, 2014, p. 1). Importantly, the discrepancy method covers a combination of estimate procedures, which may differ from country to country and the calculation method is not well documented (Schneider, 2017). To explain the significant differences between the NOE estimates and the MIMIC calculation one must keep in mind the double counting problem while using MIMIC method (what leads to high values). Indeed, the adjusted macro results are sometimes closer to the NOE calculation than the MIMIC estimates. The difference shrinks considerably for Poland, where the NOE and macro adjusted estimates show the similar level (15.4 vs. 16% of GDP, see Table 3.1). For Czech Republic the difference is greater (8.1% according to NOE and 10.5% according adjusted macro estimates). Nevertheless, one should take into account that there is no internationally accepted definition of shadow economy, and therefore the cross-country and methods comparisons have to be taken with caution.

Another part of estimates of the shadow economy constitute the direct measures derived from survey studies. We recall two international surveys related to informal economy. Fist of them, the Special Eurobarometer survey No. 402, conducted in 2013 is based on 26,563 face-to-face interviews in the 27 European Union. The respondents were asked, among others, whether in the past 12 months they worked without the formal written contract and if they received "envelope wages" defined as unregistered part of remuneration in formal job (European Commission, 2014). According to the Eurobarometer survey 2013 5% of dependent employees in Poland had received envelope wages in the 12 months prior to the survey, similar to Czech Republic, whereas in Slovak Republic the share amounts to 7%, in Austria 2% and in Netherlands 3%. Moreover, 2% of respondents in Poland declare a work without formal written contract, similar to Austria. The Czech Republic and Slovak Republic report no dependent employees without formal written contract. As can be seen the shares of informal activities according to Eurobarometer survey are significantly lower than the macro estimates what is typical for direct methods biased with underestimation.

Second source of direct data on shadow economy stems from the Enterprise survey conducted by World Bank and the European Bank for Reconstruction and Development (also known as Business Environment and Enterprise Performance Surveys (BEEPS)). An Enterprise Survey is a firm-level survey of a representative sample of an economy's private sector conducted in 139 countries. We report two questions from the section on informality related to informal sector as a source of unfair competition to registered enterprises. Firstly, we present the percentage of firms competing against unregistered or informal firms. The numbers for Poland, Czech Republic and Slovak Republic are alarming. Every third formal firm must face the unfair competition from informal sector. In Czech Republic and Slovak Republic the situation is even worse (36% and 42.8% of formal firms respectively). Moreover, 15.3% of formal firm in Poland (23.3% in Czech Republic and 14.6% in Slovak Republic) claims that practices of competitors in the informal sector constitutes a major constraint in running the business.

Besides the international sources also the national data on shadow economy in Poland are available. In so far, there have been just few attempts to estimate the size of the shadow economy in Poland. Relatively the earliest (for the period between 1991 and 1995) estimates of the size of shadow economy in Poland are provided by Lackó (1999). According to her estimates based on power energy consumption in 1991 the size of the shadow economy achieved 33% of national GDP. In consecutive 2 years it was dropping by 1% p.p. annually, then in 1994 it was 28% and in 1995—24%. Next, in Schneider and Raczkowski (2013) again we find estimates that coincide with these reported in Schneider (2015).

In Table 3.3 we compile available data on shadow economy and informal employment calculations in Poland. Polish national accounts provided by Central Statistical Office (CSO) include two parts of unofficial economy: the hidden part which is legal but the economic activities are concealed from relevant authorities and the totally illegal economy. The hidden economy is divided into underreporting of economic activities (underreporting of production and VAT fraud) in registered entities (all companies up to 9 employees and private companies with 10–49 employees) and unregistered work performed by natural persons. Yearly estimates provided by Central Statistical Office in Poland (CSO) are based on several data sources: direct method, studies on unregistered work (Labour Force Survey and The Module Survey Unregistered Employment), consumer survey and estimates of activities related to the provision of sexual services. Besides those estimates since 2010 the CSO also has provided the measures on illegal economy, which includes pimping, drugs and cigarettes smuggling. Illegal activities amounted to 0.7% of GDP in 2010 and 2011 and 0.8% of GDP in 2012 and 2013 and 0.6% in 2014. The share of hidden economy in Poland has shown slightly declining trend since the year 2000 (17% of GDP in 2000 versus 12.7 in 2014). Moreover, the majority of hidden business activities took place in registered entities (10.4% in 2014) whereas the undeclared work conducted by natural persons by their own account amounted to 2.3% in 2014. This means that practices like underreporting of production and VAT fraud in legal companies are prevalent in Poland and constitute a significant part of the shadow economy. Moreover, among the most affected sectors one may mention trade and repair of motor vehicles, accommodation and catering (5.8% in 2014) and construction (2.3% in 2014). According to another research on shadow economy conducted by the Gdansk Institute for Market Economics (IBnGR), the extent of shadow economy in Poland is greater than reported by CSO. The estimates provided by IBnGR since 2010 include also illegal activities and a part of informal activities, which are not included by Central Statistical Office (the precise list of additional components is to find in (Łapiński, Peterlik, & Wyżnikiewicz, 2015, p. 25–26). According to

Table 3.3 Estimates of shadow economy share and informal employment in Poland

Source	Types of estimates	2000	2001	2002	2003	2004	2005	2006	2007	2008	2009	2010	2011	2012	2013	2014	2015	2016
Central Statistical Office (CSO)	Shadow economy as % GDP	17.0	16.8	15.4	15.8	14.5	15.9	15.9	12.8	11.8	13.1	12.8	11.9	12.2	13.0	12.7	13.2	
	In registered entities	11.7	11.6	10.2	10.7	9.6	11.0	11.2	9.2	8.3	9.6	9.5	8.8	9.6	10.6	10.4	11.0	
	In respect of undeclared work	5.3	5.2	5.2	5.1	4.9	4.9	4.7	3.6	3.5	3.5	3.3	2.4	2.6	2.4	2.3	2.2	
Research Institute for Market Economy (IBnGR)	Shadow economy as % of GDP											21	20	21.1	19.9	19.5	19.2	19.7
Module Survey Unregistered Employment	Unregistered employment % of the total number of employed			14.9 (1995)	9.3 (1998)	9.6					4.9	4.6				4.5		
Yearly indirect estimates provided by CSO	Share of workers in shadow economy in total employment	5.71	5.97	7.11	7.31	7.68	8.03	8.24	8.21	8.32	8.32	7.61	7.66	7.71	7.52	6.87	6.54	
Human Capital Balance	Direct estimates of share of working without written contract											4.7	4.1	3.8	3.8	4.0		

Source: (CSO, 2008, 2015a, 2016), (Fundowicz et al., 2016; Łapiński et al., 2015), Statistical Yearbooks of the Republic of Poland for the years 2001–2016 (CSO), (CSO, 2015b)

those calculations the share of unofficial economy (both legal and illegal) amounted to about 20% of GDP what significantly exceeds the estimates provided by CSO (according to which in 2014 the share of shadow economy is 12.7% of GDP). On the other hand those estimates are a little closer to the level of calculation of the index of shadow economy based on company managers and Schneider's estimates.

Another part of estimates provided by CSO includes the calculations of informal (unregistered) employment. So far there are two available sources of statistics based on two different methods. First of them are indirect estimates provided on yearly basis in the Statistical Yearbooks of the Republic of Poland and include studies of work in registered enterprises and public budget entities, studies on registered unemployment (number of people registered as unemployed in labor offices), Labour Force Survey - LFS and the Module Survey Unregistered Employment. In Table 3.3 we present the calculations of the share of employment in shadow economy to the total employment. Informal employees constitute about 6–8% of total number of employees and the level of informality is stable since 2002. A second source of estimates are based on direct calculations coming from a cyclical Module Survey Unregistered Employment conducted parallel to the Labour Force Survey in Poland. So far, six surveys were carried out (in 1995, 1998, 2004, 2009, 2010, 2014). The study describes the scale of undeclared work, which includes an employment without an employment relationship, social insurance and counted contribution period, with the lack of income taxes and in case of self-employment (CSO, 2011). Analyzing the data from module survey we observe a declining trend since the year 1995. In 2014 compared to 1995, the number of informal workers dropped by almost 1.5 million. Importantly, the estimates from Module Survey show a lower level of informal workers than the yearly estimates what is typical for direct methods. People engaged in shadow economy are not willing to tell the truth and therefore the surveys indicate the lower boundary of informality.

Apart from the estimates provided by CSO Polish Agency for Enterprise Development in cooperation with the Jagiellonian University in Krakov conduct independent research covering shadow economy aspects. The survey study called Human Capital Balance has been carried out since 2010 and refers to the structure of competences available in the labour market in Poland. The data provided on yearly bases are available online at https://bkl.parp.gov.pl/dane.html. The scope of this study is wide and the questionnaire of population module consists of several parts referring i.a. to present and past employment. In order to indicate the prevalence of informal jobs one of the question is: *Have you worked on the basis of an informal agreement, e.g. a verbal agreement, in the past 12 months?* The direct estimates of the share of informal employment are presented in Table 3.3. The latest available results from 2014 show that about 4% of respondents worked informally. Those estimates therefore are in line with the Module Survey conducted by CSO.

References

Arendt, L., Grabowski, W., & Kukulak-Dolata, I. (2020). County-level patterns of undeclared work: An empirical analysis of a highly diversified region in the European Union. *Social Indicators Research, 149*(1), 271–295. https://doi.org/10.1007/s11205-019-02243-4

Beręsewicz, M., & Nikulin, D. (2019). *Estimation of the size of informal employment based on administrative records with non-ignorable selection mechanism.* https://doi.org/10.13140/RG.2.2.34792.11522

Buehn, A., & Schneider, F. (2012). *Shadow economies in highly developed OECD countries: What are the driving forces?* (IZA Discussion Paper). Retrieved from http://ideas.repec.org/p/jku/econwp/2013_17.html

Cagan, P. (1958). The demand for currency relative to the total money supply. *Journal of Political Economy, 66*(4), 303–328.

CSO. (2008). *National accounts by institutional sectors and sub-sectors 2000-2006*. Warsaw.

CSO. (2011). *Unregistered employment in Poland in 2010.*

CSO. (2015a). *National Accounts by institutional sectors and sub-sectors 2010-2013*. Warsaw.

CSO. (2015b). *Unregistered employment in Poland in 2014, Central Statistical Office, Demographic and Labour Market Surveys Department*. Warsaw: Central Statistical Office. https://doi.org/10.1017/CBO9781107415324.004

CSO. (2016). *National accounts by institutional sectors and sub-sectors 2011-2014*. Warsaw.

Di Caro, P., & Nicotra, G. (2016). Short, long and spatial dynamics of informal employment. *Regional Studies, 50*(11), 1804–1818. https://doi.org/10.1080/00343404.2015.1072274

Di Porto, E. (2011). Audit, tax compliance and undeclared work. *Public Finance Review, 39*(1), 75–102. https://doi.org/10.1177/1091142110381641

Dybka, P., Kowalczuk, M., Olesiński, B., Torój, A., & Rozkrut, M. (2019). Currency demand and MIMIC models: Towards a structured hybrid method of measuring the shadow economy. *International Tax and Public Finance, 26*(1), 4–40. https://doi.org/10.1007/s10797-018-9504-5.

European Commission. (2014). *Undeclared work in the European Union. Special Eurobarometer 402*. Brussels: European Commission. https://doi.org/10.2767/37041

European Commission. (2020). *Special Eurobarometer 498. Undeclared work in the European Union*. Retrieved from https://ec.europa.eu/commfrontoffice/publicopinion/index.cfm/Survey/getSurveyDetail/instruments/SPECIAL/surveyKy/2250

Feige, E. L. (1996). *Overseas holdings of US currency and the underground economy* (pp. 5–62). Kalamazoo, MI: Exploring the Underground Economy.

Feld, L., & Larsen, C. (2009). *Undeclared work in Germany 2001-2007—Impact of deterrence, tax policy, and social norms: An analysis based on survey data*. Berlin: Springer.

Feld, L. P., & Schneider, F. (2017). Reply to Gebhard Kirchgässner. *German Economic Review, 18*(1), 112–117. https://doi.org/10.1111/geer.12097

Fundowicz, J., Łapiński, K., Peterlik, M., & Wyżnikiewicz, B. (2016). *Szara strefa w polskiej gospodarce w 2016 roku*. Warszawa.

Gërxhani, K. (2007). "Did you pay your taxes?" How (not) to conduct tax evasion surveys in transition countries. *Social Indicators Research, 80*(3), 555–581. https://doi.org/10.1007/s11205-006-0007-x

Groves, R. M. (2006). Nonresponse rates and nonresponse bias in household surveys. *Public Opinion Quarterly, 70*(5), 646–675. https://doi.org/10.1093/poq/nfl033

Gutmann, P. M. (1977). The subterranean economy. *Financial Analysts Journal, 33*(6), 26–27.

Gyomai, G., & van de Ven, P. (2014). The non-observed economy in the system of national accounts. *OECD Statistics Brief.*

Heyes, J., & Hastings, T. (2017). *The practices of enforcement bodies in detecting and preventing bogus self-employment.*

Kaliberda, A., & Kaufmann, D. (1996). *Integrating the unofficial economy into the dynamics of post-socialist economies: A framework of analysis and evidence*. Geneva: The World Bank.

Kriz, K. A., Meriküll, J., Paulus, A., & Staehr, K. (2008). Why do individuals evade payroll and income taxation in Estonia? In M. Pickhardt & E. Shinnick (Eds.), *Shadow economy, corruption and governance* (pp. 240–264). Cheltenham: Edward Elgar Publishing. Retrieved from http://papers.ssrn.com/sol3/papers.cfm?abstract_id=968829

Lackó, M. (1999). *Do power consumption data tell the story? Electricity intensity and hidden economy in post-socialist countries*. Budapest Working Papers on the Labour Market.

Łapiński, K., Peterlik, M., & Wyżnikiewicz, B. (2015). *Szara strefa w polskiej gospodarce w 2015 roku*.

Lehmann, H. (2015). Informal employment in transition countries: Empirical evidence and research challenges. *Comparative Economic Studies, 57*, 1–30.

Meriküll, J., & Staehr, K. (2010). Unreported employment and envelope wages in mid-transition: Comparing developments and causes in the baltic countries. *Comparative Economic Studies, 52*(4), 637–670. https://doi.org/10.1057/ces.2010.17

Nikulin, D., & Sobiechowska-Ziegert, A. (2018). Informal work in Poland—A regional approach. *Papers in Regional Science, 97*(4), 1227–1246. https://doi.org/10.1111/pirs.12306

Schneider, F. (2015). Size and development of the shadow economy of 31 European and 5 other OECD Countries from 2003 to 2014: Different developments? *Journal of Self-Governance and Management Economics, 3*(4), 7–29.

Schneider, F. (2016). *Size and development of the shadow economy of 31 European and 5 other OECD countries from 2003 to 2012: Some new facts*. http://www.econ.jku.at/members/Schneider/files/publications/2012/ShadEcEurope31.pdf. Retrieved February, from http://www.econ.jku.at/schneider

Schneider, F. (2017). *Implausible large differences of the size of the underground economies in highly developed European countries? A comparison of different estimation methods*.

Schneider, F. (2019). Size of the shadow economies of 28 European Union countries from 2003 to 2018. The latest development. In V. Vlachos & A. Bitzenis (Eds.), *European Union post crisis challenges and prospects for growth* (pp. 111–121). Cham: Palgrave Macmillan.

Schneider, F., & Buehn, A. (2017). Shadow economy: Estimation methods, problems, results and open questions. *Open Economics, 1*(1), 1–29. https://doi.org/10.1515/openec-2017-0001

Schneider, F., Buehn, A., & Montenegro, C. E. (2010). New estimates for the shadow economies all over the world. *International Economic Journal, 24*(July), 443–461. https://doi.org/10.1080/10168737.2010.525974.

Schneider, F., Buehn, A., & Schneider, F. (2007). Shadow economies and corruption all over the world: Revised estimates for 120 countries. *Economics. The Open-Access, Open-Assessment E-Journal, 1*, 1–53. https://doi.org/10.5018/economics-ejournal.ja.2007-9

Schneider, F., & Enste, D. H. (2000). Shadow economies: Size, causes, and consequences. *Journal of Economic Literature, XXXVIII*(March), 77–114. https://doi.org/10.1257/jel.38.1.77

Schneider, F., & Enste, D. H. (2013). *The shadow economy: An international survey*. Cambridge: Cambridge University Press.

Schneider, F., & Raczkowski, K. (2013). Size and development of the shadow economy and of tax evasion within Poland and of its neighbouring countries from 2003 to 2013: Some new facts. In *The economic security of business transactions. Management in business* (pp. 3–31). Oxford: Chartridge Books Oxford.

Schneider, F., & Williams, C. C. (2013). *The shadow economy*. London: The Institute of Economic Affairs.

Tanzi, V. (1980). The underground economy in the United States: Estimates and implications. *PSL Quarterly Review, 33*(135), 427–453.

Zukauskas, V., & Schneider, F. (2016). Microbased results of shadow labour market in the Baltic States, Poland and Sweden. *Applied Economics: Systematic Research, 10*(2), 117–133.

Chapter 4
Shadow Economy in Poland: Results of the Survey

Abstract In this chapter we present the empirical findings from the company survey conducted among representative sample of polish companies. Firstly, we provide the description of the materials and methods applied, needed to understand the approach we employ. Then, we follow the methodology proposed by Putniņš & Sauka (Journal of Comparative Economics 43:471–490, 2015) in order to estimate the extent of shadow economy in Poland. As the final results we present the Index of the Shadow Economy which indicates the prevalence of informal activities in Poland. Afterwards, we analyze the reasons and factors which may impact the desire for being involved in shadow economy and conducting informal activities. Following the theoretical background we derive a set of determinants of the shadow economy. In particular, we recall the approaches which assert the importance of institutional environment, tax severity and tax morality in explaining the extent of the shadow economy.

4.1 Materials and Methods

As the empirical evidence on the extent and prevalence of informal activities is still limited, there is a need for further research which will deliver necessary empirical material. To meet these limitations we provide an own survey results dedicated to shadow economy. The survey on shadow economy in Poland was conducted in April 2017 on behalf on the Faculty of Management and Economics, Gdańsk University of Technology in Poland by the data collecting company. The survey is aiming at the understanding of entrepreneurs' satisfaction with entrepreneurship climate in Poland. The research schedule as well as questionnaire form is based on the similar survey conducted in Baltic states since 2010 by Putniņš and Sauka (2015) and is presented in Appendix A. The survey is based on the computer assisted telephone interviews (CATI). The respondents cover company owners or alternatively high level managers. The final survey sample consists of 454 representative polish enterprises. For the representativeness purpose random stratified sample was used with three strata: voivodship (statistical region NUTS 2: according to the Nomenclature of Territorial Units for Statistics), industry (five main sectors: manufacturing, wholesale, retail, services and construction) and employment size (0–9,

D. Nikulin, E. Lechman, *Shadow Economy in Poland*, SpringerBriefs in Economics, https://doi.org/10.1007/978-3-030-70524-4_4

10–49 and 50–249 employees). The detailed sample description is included in Appendix B.

The survey consists of four sections: (1) external influences, (2) government policy and amount of informal business, (3) company, performance, value creation and (4) attitudes, tax morale, barriers to business. The scope of the survey enables to analyze the issue of entrepreneurship with the focus on informal part of them from many sides. In the first part, the possible barriers impacting the business are indicated. This section consists of questions on the satisfaction with the State Revenue Service, government's tax policy, quality of business legislation and support to entrepreneurs in Poland. Moreover, the respondents are asked about the tolerance towards tax avoidance and bribing. In this way, the institutional background of polish entrepreneurship serves as an introduction to the analysis of bigger obstacles and problems. Importantly, the entrepreneurs' social norms may play an important role in explaining the propensity to involvement in the shadow economy activities (Torgler, 2007). Moreover, the gradual approach in surveys of sensitive topics is recommended in order to enhance the response rate and truthfulness of responses. This strategy is often used if the questions are of thorny nature and the respondents are not willing to clear response (Tourangeau & Yan, 2007). By starting with questions on problems they are struggling with, we enhance the willingness of participating in the survey, as respondents may start to identify with these obstacles. Additionally, we title this survey as "Identification of Barriers to Entrepreneurship in Poland" instead of a survey on informal activities, in order to not to discourage respondents to participate in the survey.

In the second section of this survey, the questions asked aim to quantify the amount of informal activities in Poland through assessing the prevalence of underreporting business income, underreporting the number of employees, underreporting the salaries as well as calculating the extent of unofficial payments to "get things done" or to "secure the contract". In addition, the respondents were asked to assess the probability of being caught while operating informally and the consequences of that. In this way, this set of questions aims to assess the extent of different forms of underreporting. As the straightforward questions on informal activities are very sensitive, it is postulated to using the indirect way of asking. In this survey, we follow the suggestion from Sauka (2008) and ask the respondents about the estimated extent of underreporting in firms in their industry, instead of in their own firm. As Sauka (2008) argues, the answers are similar in both cases, if the respondents are asked about the underreporting in their firms, as well as in firms in their industry. This technique aims to increase the number of truthful answers and at the same time, to decrease the extent of refusal. The justification found in the literature asserts moreover that the correlation between perceived tax evasion in the reference group and the self-reported tax evasion is significant (Webley, Cole, & Eidjar, 2001). Similarly, Gérxhani (2007) claims that the indirect way of asking may be used instead of the respondent's own answer. As the common bias in survey based research is the risk of underestimation, this approach minimize this danger by using the above mentioned techniques created for sensitive nature of the topic.

In the third section of the survey the companies' performances are reported including operating profits, turnovers, numbers of employees as well as the sector and place of main activity. This information is gathered to quantify the financial achievements of surveyed enterprises, which, in turn, are needed to calculate the proportion of undeclared activities in the total business activities. Additionally, the data on the sector of the main activity and the localization of the company provide necessary information to deeper analyzes of the phenomenon of shadow economy.

The fourth part of this survey is on attitudes describing the inclination towards tax compliance, the tax morality and perceived barriers which hamper the development of a business. In particular, the respondents indicate their assessment of contribution to the growth of the polish economy and society and the feeling to belong to the local community. Moreover they gauge the justification for cheating on taxes. Further, the factors which may affect the current operations in the company are indicated. This set of questions is of particular importance as recently, the role of perceived fairness of the tax system and social norms is underlined (Kogler, Muehlbacher, & Kirchler, 2015). In particular, the social norms related to the tax morale are mentioned as an important factor in explaining informal activities (for a review, see Ahmed & Braithwaite, 2005). Another strand of research show that the social norms towards informal activities may be correlated with general norms in a given social group (Webley et al., 2001).

To sum up, the survey material provides a good source of data, which may be used to analyze the shadow economy in a broader sense. A diverse character of questions enables not only the calculation of the extent of the informal activities but also to investigate their causes, what is the main content of this book. In the subsequent sections we present the results of the construction of the Shadow Economy Index in Poland, which quantify the extent of shadow economy as well as the reasons for being involved in the shadow economy.

4.2 Shadow Economy Index: Estimates for Poland

The construction of Shadow Economy Index is a proposition of measuring informal economy using the direct methods. The idea of calculation the size of informal economy has been developed in Baltic states since 2010 (Sauka & Putniņš, 2016). In this study we follow the methodology proposed by Putniņš and Sauka (2015) in order to construct the index for the years 2015 and 2016. The shadow economy index is measured as the share of the shadow economy in Gross Domestic Product (GDP) calculated with the income approach. Importantly, as the capacity of the "shadow economy" term is very broad, in this approach only the legal production of goods and services concealed from public authorities is taken into account. In this way, the important information about the extent and nature of informal activities will be provided, what may facilitate the implementation of justified policy measures.

As described in Putniņš and Sauka (2015) the construction of shadow economy index consists of three steps. In the first stage three types of underreporting are taken into account: underreporting of business income, underreporting of number of employees and underreporting of salaries paid to employees. The exact values of this rations are derived from questions Q7, Q8 and Q9 from the questionnaire (see Appendix A). Therefore, the extent of the shadow economy covers this three elements, what is in line with the recent approach in measuring the informal activities, based on their heterogeneous character (European Commission, 2020).

Based on the estimated shares of underreporting activities, in particular the unreported number of employees and the salaries, a proportion of unreported employee remuneration (UER) in each firm *i* is calculated following the formula (4.1).

$$\mathrm{UER}_{\mathrm{i}} = 1 - \left(1 - \text{underreported salaries}_{\mathrm{i}}\right)\left(1 - \text{underreported employees}_{\mathrm{i}}\right) \quad (4.1)$$

where:

underreported salaries: the share of underreported salary in the total salary in given firm *i*;
underreported employees: the share of informal employment in total employment in given firm *i*.

The Fig. 4.1 presents the share of informal activities in Poland indicated by the respondents.

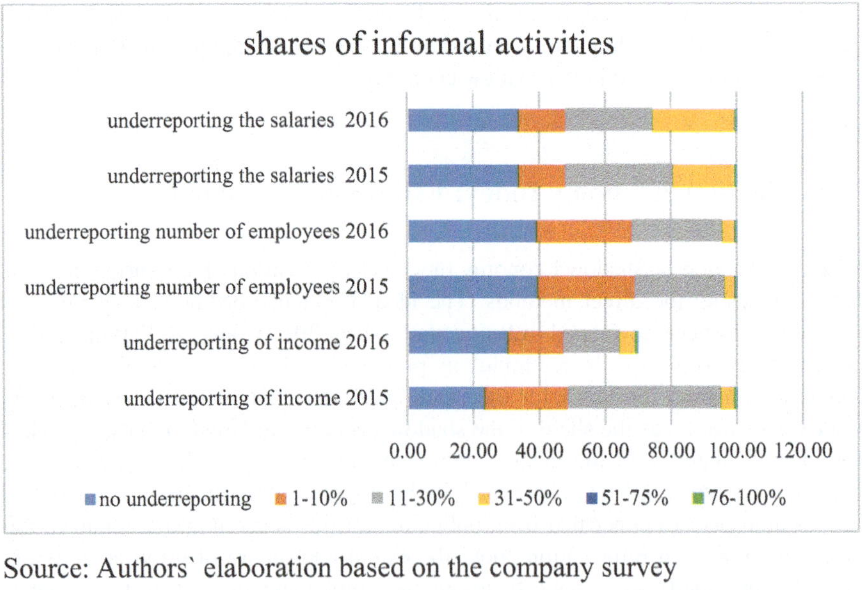

Fig. 4.1 Informal activities in polish companies. Source: Authors' elaboration based on the company survey

As derived from Fig. 4.1 an significant part of polish entrepreneurs indicates a considerable extent of unreported activities. Going into details, only 30% of company managers declares no underreporting of income in 2016 (23% in 2015), almost 40% admits no unreported employees and 34% points no degree of unreported salaries. The remaining part of entrepreneurs declare some degree of underreporting, while in case of salaries (which are paid in form of envelope wages), the almost one fifth companies indicates the understating the real salaries of 31–50%. This facts are alarming, and motivate to further calculations of the extent of shadow activities in Poland.

As the next step, we compute the shadow proportion for each firms *i* which is composed of the sum of unreported employee remuneration and the underreported operating income using the formula (4.2). As Putniņš and Sauka (2015) postulate, in order to interpret the shadow economy index in relation of Gross Domestic Product, there is a need to consider the ratio of employee remuneration in the total sum of employee remuneration and company income. To do this we use the ratio of compensation of employees provided by Eurostat (Eurostat item D.1) to the sum of employees' remuneration and gross operating surplus and mixed income of firms (Eurostat items B.2g and B.3g). For the year 2015 as well as for 2016 the ratio (α) is amounted to 42% for Poland.

$$\text{shadow proportion}_{\text{it}} = \alpha \text{ UER}_{\text{i}} + (1-\alpha) \text{ underreported income}_{\text{i}} \qquad (4.2)$$

where:

i—firm;
t—year;
α—the ratio of employee compensation to the sum of employee compensation and company income, derived from Eurostat.

Having the proportions of shadow economy for each firm, we are able to calculate the Shadow Economy Index for Poland, for the year 2015 and 2016. To do this we use the relative contribution of each firm to the country's GDP approximate the weights using the number of employees in each company (Q18). In this way we obtain the Shadow Economy Index, which represents a share of shadow economy as a share of the whole economy. As a result we receive the Shadow Economy Index in Poland as 24.47% of GDP in 2015 and 24.98% of GDP in 2016.

As similar estimates were previously calculated in Baltic states, obviously we aim to confront the shadow index for Poland with other countries. Comparing our results with the results obtained for Estonia, Latvia and Lithuania we observe that the share of shadow economy in Poland is the highest. According to the last report on Baltic countries the shadow economies in Estonia account for 15.4%, in Lithuania 16.5% and in Latvia 20.3% of GDP in 2016. (Putniņš & Sauka, 2017). The reason for these disparities may be due to the differences in the share of the small enterprises in the total number of enterprises. According to Eurostat[1] the participation of

[1] https://ec.europa.eu/eurostat/en/web/products-eurostat-news/-/ddn-20200514-1

the small enterprises in the total economy is the highest in Poland (98.9% in comparison to 98.4% in Estonia, 98.7% in Lithuania and 98.6% in Latvia in 2017). The remaining differences may be partially explained by the driving forces for informal activities, which are discussed in the next section.

Gong further it seems to be reasonable to compare our results with remaining estimates of the extent of the shadow economy in Poland. However, the simple comparison is not possible, as our estimates are the first based on the company survey. Interestingly, the share of shadow economy calculated from managers' survey as almost 25% of GDP (in 2015 and 2016) exceeds the estimates of Schneider according to MIMIC methodology (23% in 2016). Obviously, another estimates show even lower extent of shadow economy. Adjusted macro calculation are close to NOE estimates provided by OECD (16% and 15.4% of GDP in 2012 respectively). Invoking on national sources the highest level of shadow economy is presented in the statistics calculated by Gdansk Institute for Market Research (19.5% of GDP in 2014) which covers additional economy areas (like illegal fuel trade, part of marketplace trade, part of cross-border trade or the dynamically growing e-commerce) which are not included in the estimates provided by the Statistics Poland. The estimates made by Statistics Poland, therefore, are considerably lower (12.4% of GDP in 2014). Recent estimates, in turn, conducted by the Statistics Poland and expanded by the Institute of Economic Forecasts and Analyses (see Fundowicz, 2020) show that the share of the shadow economy in the adjusted polish GDP accounts 17.4% in 2020. Those estimates cover three main elements: the illegal part (like the pimping, drug production and trafficking or cigarette smuggling), hidden activities (e.g. those conducted in registered part of the economy) and the purely informal activities (not registered). Since our estimates are related mainly to the underreporting of the activities and therefore may be described as the hidden activities in registered entities, we may claim that the existing estimates derived from national accounts are underestimated. Given the fact, that in case of our calculations, the extent of the shadow economy is likely to be underestimated (what is typical for survey studies on shadow economy), the real extent of the shadow economy could be even much higher. Obviously, it is impossible to directly compare available estimates due to the different methodology approach used, but it is important to be aware of the existing differences and possible underestimations of the extent of the shadow economy provided in the national statistics.

4.3 Tracing the Root Causes of the Shadow Economy in Poland

Besides the estimates of the extent of the shadow economy it is equally important to know the factors which impact the probability of being involved in informal activities. Based on our company managers survey conducted in 2017 including questions on entrepreneurs' satisfaction with entrepreneurship climate and informal activities several factors influencing informal side of the economy may be detected. According to the survey questionnaire and the methodology proposed by

Mickiewicz, Rebmann, and Sauka (2017) the reasons for going underground may be divided into: normative, cognitive and regulatory. In Table 4.1 we compile questions and answers referring to those three pillars to show the opinion on business climate in Poland. Questions A and B cover the field of confidence in tax authorities and confidence in government (normative perspective), question C refers to the identification with the local community (cognitive perspective), questions D and E include, in turn, deterrence issues (regulatory perspective).

According to the above results, most of company managers declare their dissatisfaction both with the State Revenue Service and government's tax policy what may motivate their attitude towards tax evasion. The existing empirical evidence suggests a relationship between the quality of institutions and the size of shadow economy, The cross-country study from Torgler and Schneider (2007) reveals that the institutional quality significantly impact the size of the shadow economy. Similarly, Hanousek and Palda (2004), employing data for Czech and Slovak Republics, Hungary and Poland, claim that the citizens' perception of the quality of government services is an relevant determinant of the tax evasion. Barone and Mocetti (2011), in turn, using data for Italy find a positive relation between the

Table 4.1 Questions on business climate in Poland

	1	2	3	4	5	6
A. Please evaluate your satisfaction with the performance of the State Revenue Service with regards to tax administration (1—very unsatisfied, 2—unsatisfied, 3—neither satisfied nor unsatisfied, 4—satisfied, 5—very satisfied)						
	1.2%	41.44%	43.84%	12.61%	0.90%	–
B. Please evaluate your satisfaction with the government's tax policy in Poland. (1— very unsatisfied, 2—unsatisfied, 3—neither satisfied nor unsatisfied, 4—satisfied, 5—very satisfied)						
	6.01%	57.96%	34.53%	1.50%	0.00%	–
C. Being a member of the local community is important to me (1—strongly disagree, 2—disagree, 3—neither/nor, 4—agree, 5—strongly agree)						
	0.00%	2.7%	9.61%	75.08%	12.61%	–
D. For a typical company in your industry, what would you say is the approximate probability of being caught if the company were to: (1 = no chances that will be caught, 2 = 1–10% chance that will be caught, 3 = 11–30%, 4 = 31–50%, 5 = 51–75%, 6 = 76–100%)						
(i) Underreport its business income?	1.80%	2.70%	6.01%	51.35%	24.62%	13.51%
(ii) Underreport its number of employees?	1.80%	3.00%	10.21%	50.45%	21.02%	13.51%
(iii) Underreport the amount it pays to employees in salaries?	1.80%	2.70%	6.01%	51.35%	24.62%	13.51%
(iv) Make unofficial payments to 'get things done'?	3.30%	6.61%	15.02%	47.75%	16.22%	11.11%
E. If a company in your industry were caught for deliberate misreporting, what would typically be the consequence to that company?(1—Nothing serious, 2—A small fine, 3—A serious fine that would affect the competitiveness of the company, 4—A serious fine that would put the company at risk of insolvency, 5—The company would be forced to cease operations)						
	–	1.86%	35.71%	45.03%	17.39%	–

Source: Authors' elaboration based on company survey

efficiency of spending public money and attitude towards tax compliance. As we found that about 43% of respondents are very unsatisfied or unsatisfied with the performance of the institutions, while another 43% of them is neither satisfied nor unsatisfied, this may suggests, that a poor institutional environment may impact the desire to being involved in the shadow economy.

Similarly, the respondents show a high dissatisfaction with the quality of business legislation and satisfaction with the governments' support to entrepreneurs (Fig. 4.2).

The above mentioned two elements are essential for doing business as they predetermine the environment quality for entrepreneurship in a country. Business legislation defines legal framework for companies operation and activities; while governments' support to entrepreneurs may effectively boost entrepreneurial activities on economically crucial branches. We might argue that entrepreneurs' dissatisfaction with legal frameworks as well as lack of state support for companies may encourages entrepreneurs to operate on in the shadow. According to the survey, almost 60% of respondents declares to be unsatisfied with the quality of business legislation, while another 39% claims to be neither satisfied nor satisfied. Henceforth, we might suppose that barely 92% of respondents were poorly satisfied with the quality of business legislation. The latter suggests that entrepreneurs in Poland basically feel oppressed with the poor quality legal framework, which in turn may be perceived as the factor "making it easy" to go into shadow economy. These results coincide with the responses obtained for the question on entrepreneurs' satisfaction

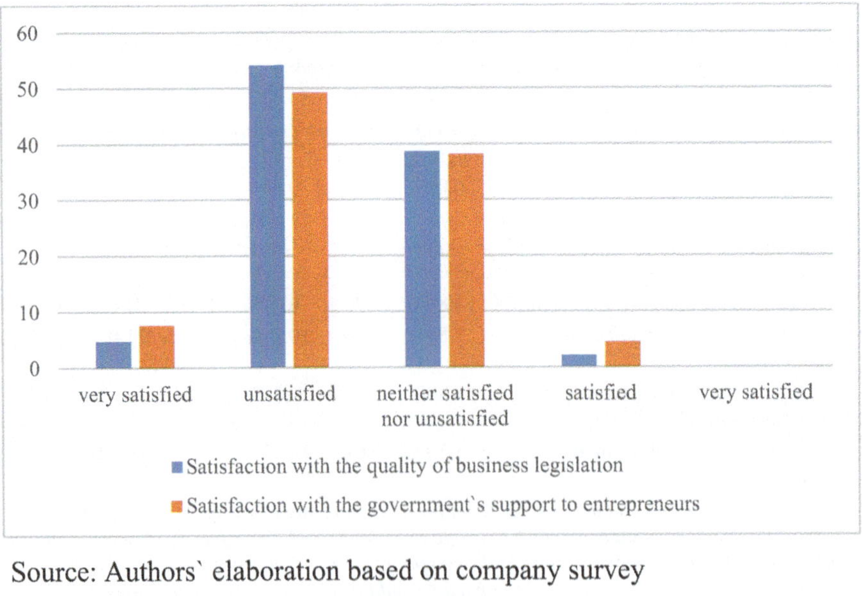

Fig. 4.2 Satisfaction with the business legislation and government support to entrepreneurs. Source: Authors' elaboration based on company survey

with the government support. Almost a half of surveyed, entrepreneurs felt unsatisfied with the government support and another 43% – felt neither satisfied nor unsatisfied. This shows that nearly 90% of entrepreneurs questioned felt that in Poland state policies towards enterprise sector support is poor and does not constitute an important incentive for starting and/or doing own business.

Going further, a common approach in the literature asserts that the lower the tax morality the higher the inclination to evade taxes and the level of engagement in the shadow activities (see i.a. Torgler & Schneider, 2009). Importantly, nowadays, the social and moral determinants of being involved in informal activities are becoming more and more important. In particular, it is claimed that non-economic social factors are relevant for explaining the inclination to be engaged in the shadow economy (Pickhardt & Prinz, 2014) as the attitudes towards playing taxes play significant role in tax compliance. Empirical evidence in this matter shows that personal moral norms as well as the norms attributed to people from the immediate surroundings may create the taxpayers' behaviour (Bobek, Roberts, & Sweeney, 2007; Kogler et al., 2013). Importantly, empirical studies confirm the relationship between tax morality (described as intrinsic motivation of pay taxes (Torgler & Schneider, 2007) or as "a belief in contributing to society by paying taxes" (Torgler & Schneider, 2009, p. 230) and the tendency to evade taxes (Alm & Torgler, 2006; Krasniqi & Williams, 2017; Torgler & Schneider, 2009). In this light the general dissatisfaction among company managers with the government and tax authorietes may influnce their tax morality and therefore increase their propensity do evade taxes. Therefore, analyzing the answers presented in Table 4.1, some initial conclusions on the negative impact on tax morale on underreporting probability may be drawn.

Next, we relate three another questions which may indicate the attitude of taxpayer towards the tax compliance: (1) *Tax avoidance is tolerated behavior in Poland*, (2) *Bribing is tolerated behavior in Poland*, (3) *Companies in your industry would think it is always justified to cheat on tax if they have the chance*. Answers to the above questions are coded according to 5 point Likert scale: strongly disagree, disagree, neither agree nor disagree, agree, strongly agree. Figure 4.3 presents the distribution of the answers.

Again, the results show that the tax morality in polish companies, reflected in the extent of the tolerance of tax avoidance, bribing and cheating on taxes, is rather on average level. Only about a half of the respondents strongly disagree with the immoral attitudes towards paying taxes. Similarly, only slightly above 50% of surveyed entrepreneurs do not confirm that bribing, a one of the channel through which the size of the shadow economy is demonstrated, is a tolerated behavior. Put differently it suggests that around 50% of respondents do not tolerate bribing as a way of doing business, which consequently might lead to the conclusion that only 50% of Polish entrepreneurs do not bribe. Similarly, barely 42% of respondents is undecided whether cheating on taxes is justified if there is a chance to do it. The 2% admit that they would cheat on tax if they had a chance. By saying so they—in fact, admit that cheating on taxes is acceptable by almost 44% of companies in the industry they operate. It shows that cheating on tax is a problem for a great share of

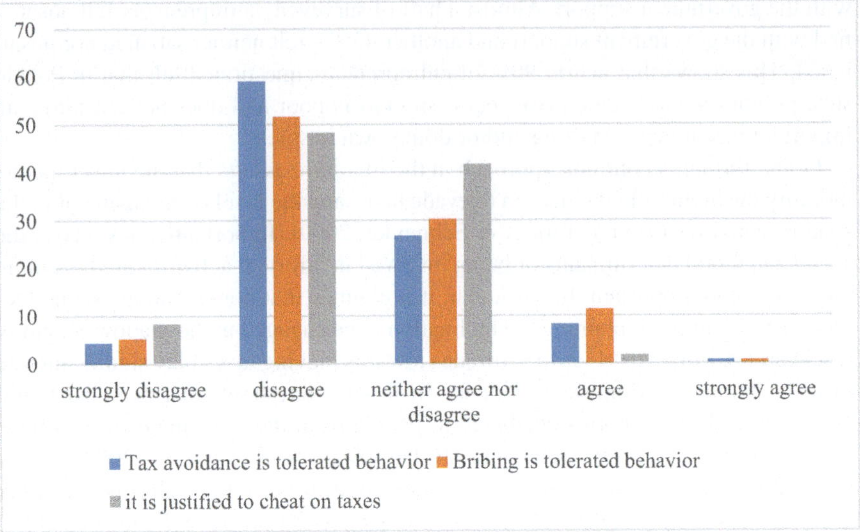

Source: Authors` elaboration based on company survey.

Fig. 4.3 Answers to tax morality related questions. Source: Authors' elaboration based on company survey

companies, and on that basis we might conclude that almost 44% of firms operate in the shadow.

Going further, the survey results show a strong identification with the local community among polish enterpreneurs (question C in Table 4.1). This should, in turn, constitutes a driving force to bigger tax compliance as people who strongly identify with the community are more inclined to contribute to the society through taxes (see i.a. Martinez-Vazquez & Torgler, 2009). In this way this strong identification with the local community may mitigate the negative impact related to the low tax morality among polish enterpreneurs. Moreover, entrepreneurs in Poland feel like 'doing a good job' both in purely economic and social terms. Figure 4.4 shows that 70% of respondents feels like their business contribute to economic and social growth. It demonstrates that surveyed entrepreneurs, despite the fact that they feel that both business legislation and state policy are basically unfavorable in terms of doing business, they feel satisfaction with running their business. These results may seem a bit contradictory at first sign, but evidently show entrepreneurs' positive attitude toward doing business.

Moreover, the individual choice on evade taxes may depend on the calculations between profits from evading taxes and risk of being caught, what is postulated in the most prevalent model based on rational choice, pioneered by Allingham and Sandmo (1972). Analysing the questions D and E (Table 4.1) we can assume that both the probability of being caught is rather high as well as the condequences in case of being caught are serious fine. In the light of the persived likelihood of being

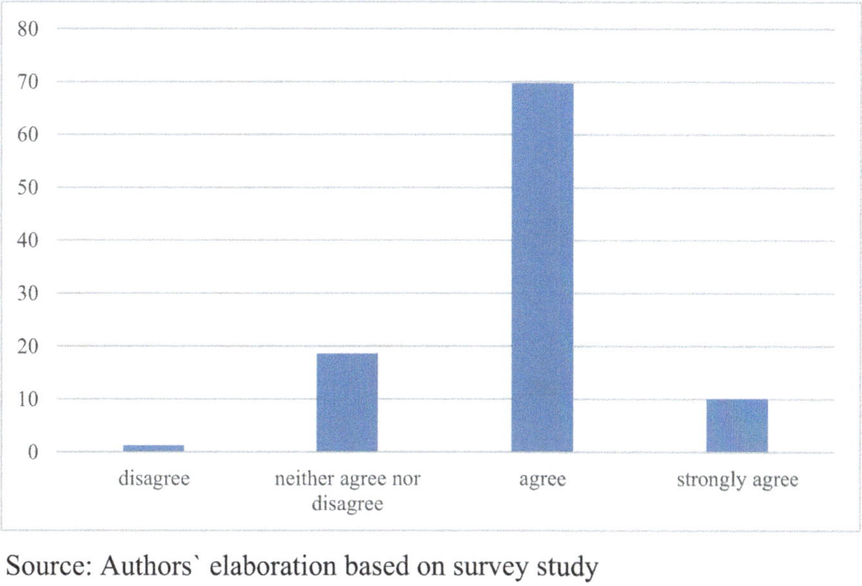

Fig. 4.4 Assessment of the business contribution to economic and social growth. Source: Authors' elaboration based on survey study

caught and severity of punishment, those factors may be therefore located among driving forces for tax evasion in Poland.

Against this backgound it is neccesary to turn into the popular assumption on the inclination for informal activities explained by the severity of taxes (Schneider, 2014). In general, the literature reports the negative impact of the tax wedge on employment (Deskar-Škrbić, Drezgić, & Šimović, 2018). The taxpayers may be more tax compliant if the tax rates are low and the tax system is perceived as fair (Mcgee & Benk, 2019) or if the perceived tax burden is high while the trust in government and the judicial system is high (Abdixhiku et al., 2017). Similarly, as Savić et al. (2015) find, countries with the more efficient tax administration have a lower level of the informal economy. However, if tax rates only are taken into account, their relation to tax avoidance is rather inconclusive (Bernasconi, Corazzini, & Seri, 2014; Joulfaian, 2009; Nur-Tegin, 2008) which implies no straightforward association between tax level and inclination to evade taxes.

In our survey we have checked for tax administration and tax rates assessment across polish entrepreneurs. Figure 4.5 shows the answers to the following question: *As I list some factors that can affect the current operations of a business, please tell me if you think that each factor is: no obstacle, a minor obstacle, a moderate obstacle, a major obstacle, or a very severe obstacle to the current operations of this establishment* with regards to the two obstacles: tax administration and tax rates.

These two aspects demonstrates to what extent the tax burden and tax administration constitute an obstacle to doing a business in Poland. Not surprisingly 56% of

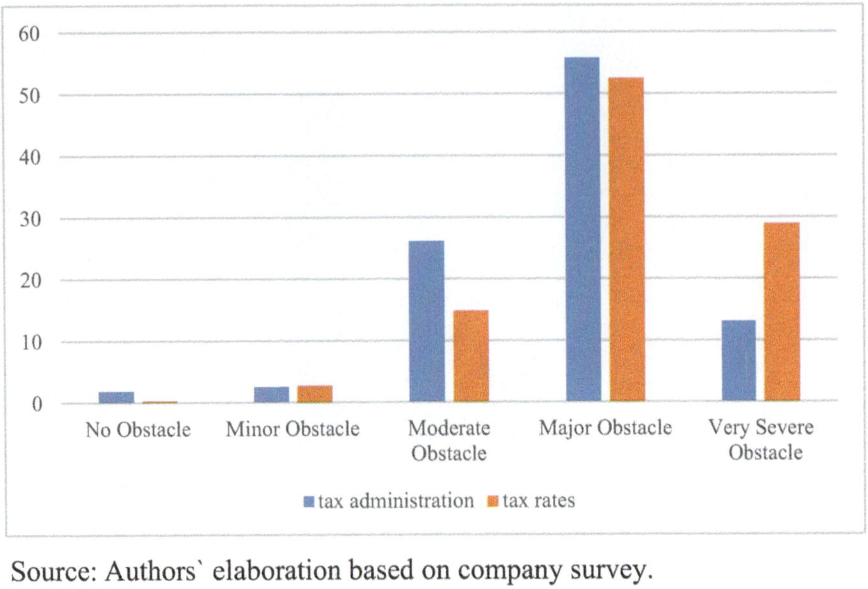

Fig. 4.5 Tax administration and tax rates as an obstacle while doing business. Source: Authors' elaboration based on company survey

respondents have indicated that tax administration is the major obstacle in doing business, while 53% have declared that the tax rates are an obstacle. For further 26% of surveyed companies tax administration constituted moderate obstacle; while around 15% of them considered tax rates as moderate obstacle. It basically shows that entrepreneurs in Poland perceive tax rates as being too high, what potentially inhibits the development of enterprises.

Moreover, as the institutional environment is becoming more and more relevant in explaining the inclination to being involved in shadow economy (Hanousek & Palda, 2004; Torgler & Schneider, 2007), below we discuss in details survey's results for the selected questions, which we believe demonstrate entrepreneurs' attitudes towards existing business environment and show their perception on major obstacles for doing business. Figure 4.6 compiles another set of institution related factors which may impact the tax payers behavior.

Following the results presented in Fig. 4.6, it seems rather logical that companies will demonstrate tendency towards tax avoidance to increase effectiveness of their business. If we add to these that more than 60% of surveyed said that trade and custom regulations, and business licensing and permits are major or very sever obstacle, henceforth it is arguable to say that legal framework in Poland is neither very favorable nor 'friendly' for entrepreneurs. Interestingly, surveyed entrepreneurs have noted that both uncertainty about regulatory policies and functioning of the judiciary system are moderate or major obstacle for running their business. Lack stability in terms of regulatory policy constitutes and important prerequisite for companies functioning, which provides long-term predictability of the business process. In fact the lack of the latter may heavily hinder long-run investment and

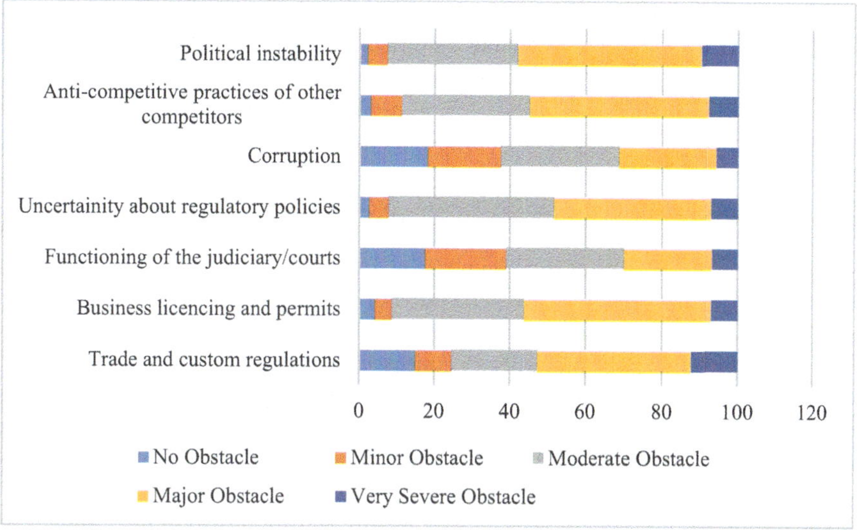

Source: Authors` elaboration based on company survey.

Fig. 4.6 Obstacles in doing busines in Poland. Source: Authors' elaboration based on company survey

strategical planning, and thus enforce companies to very limited operation in short time horizon. Similar negative effects on business development we may observe regarding the fact that barely 60% of respondents perceive poorly functioning of the judiciary system as an important obstacle in running their business. Probably entrepreneurs perceive it as a lack of legal stability and/or uncertainty, which may negatively affect their business due to—for instance—long judiciary processes. The later perfectly coincides with the results obtained for the question about 'Political instability'. In this case almost 50% of respondents have pointed the political instability as the major obstacle in doing business. This result again demonstrates that political, institutional and legal environment is decisive for how enterprises work. Finally we have tested for 'Corruption' and 'Anti-competitive practices of other competitors'. As for the first aspect almost 60% of surveyed companies declared it to be moderate or major obstacle; while 50% of respondents perceive anti-competitive practices of other companies as major obstacle in running their business.

4.4 Discussion

In the light of the foregoing, we may claim that entrepreneurs in Poland face multiple obstacles in running their business. Predominantly, the general dissatisfaction with the tax administration provided by State Revenue Service, the government's tax policy and support to entrepreneurs as well as quality of business legislation in

Poland may influence a negative attitude towards paying taxes. Following the theoretical background as well as previous empirical evidence provided in the literature, the role of quality of state institutions (Buehn & Schneider, 2012), the progressivity of taxes (Doerrenberg & Peichl, 2013), as well as the social capital and political participation (Russo, 2013) in creating the tax payers attitudes is underlined. As the citizens' perception of the quality of government services is claimed to be an important factor for tax compliance (Hanousek & Palda, 2004; Torgler & Schneider, 2007) we may consider the poor institutional environment as one of the potential driving forces for shadow economy in Poland. Importantly, the overregulation of the economy, highly correlated to the perception of the general institutional quality is a significant driving force of shadow economy. In particular, institutional measures like minimum wage or the compulsory concessions and permits allowing to conduct certain types of business may boost the informal part of labor market, what is observed in Poland. Moreover, the intricate tax system based on excessive number of forms and tax declarations discourage entrepreneurs from formal and fully registered activities. As additionally, in Poland, the transparency of economic law, and in particular of the tax system is perceived as low and the tax system is gauges as complicated, the propensity of entrepreneurs to avoid taxation is still high. Going further, the significant part of entrepreneurs perceive bribing and tax avoidance as tolerated behaviors what may be interpreted as moderate tax morale across polish companies. As it is widely argued that the decision to evade taxes may be related to the individual or social attitudes towards paying taxes, the existing social acceptance of cheating on taxes may impact the extent of shadow economy in Poland. In this way, we contribute to the previous evidence on the relationship between the tax morality and the inclination to tax evasion (Alm & Torgler, 2006; Bobek et al., 2007; Kogler et al., 2013; Krasniqi & Williams, 2017; Torgler & Schneider, 2009). Moreover, as the tax morality is defined as "a belief in contributing to society by paying taxes" (Torgler & Schneider, 2009, p. 230) and given that the quality of institutions impacts the tax morality (Buehn & Schneider, 2012), the evidence for Poland shows a negative influence from the institutional as well as from social factors on the desire to evade taxes. In general, people in Poland do not perceive the tax system as fair and they do not trust in government and the judicial system, what may implicate their lower lax compliance (Abdixhiku et al., 2017; Mcgee & Benk, 2019). Facing the excess regulations and high costs of running a business related to high tax burdens, compulsory administrative fees and the tax wedge observed in Poland the tendency of entrepreneurs to move their business to the shadow economy is high.

On the other hand, despite existing obstacles in running business in Poland, the entrepreneurs declare a significant contribution to the economic and social growth. They also underline the importance of being a member of the local community. Following the cognitive perspective proposed by Mickiewicz et al. (2017) this identification with the local community may provide to the higher tax compliance. Since, the people may be more willing to contribute to the society through taxes (see i.a. Martinez-Vazquez & Torgler, 2009), the negative impact from the low tax morality may be mitigated. The belief in the importance and contriburion of the business may be related the the influence of transformation. As at the end of the 1980s, the transformation of the social system began in Poland. In this process, political, social, economic and spatial structures changed. The impact of the transformation on the size and ownership structure of economic entities is particularly visible, which resulted in the dynamic development of small private enterprises and a significant increase in their importance in the structure of employees in the national economy. Nowadays, the micro, small and medium sized enterprises make up the bulk of the economy and their importance is still high.

Furthermore, the polish entrepreneurs are aware of the serious consequences in case of being caught on shadow activities and perceive the probability of being detected as high. Thus, based on the traditional model proposed by Allingham and Sandmo (1972) which claims that the decision the involvement in the shadow economy is related to the judgement between profits from the tax evasion and the threat to be caught, we may conclude that these factors may limit the prevalence of the shadow economy in Poland to some extent. However, as nowadays this traditional model is started to be criticized, mainly due to its simplicity (Abdixhiku et al., 2017), we are inclined to argue that the remaining other factors like institutional, tax morality and social norms related are the major driving forces of shadow economy in Poland. Following Torgler and Schneider (2009) who argue that besides the factors like tax burden, rate of public expenditure, or the density of regulation, also the "subjective perceptions, expectations, attitudes and motivations such as tax morale or the (perceived) institutional quality" (Torgler & Schneider, 2009, p. 229) should be taken into account, we underline the importance of these non-economic determinants in explaining the extent of the shadow economy. This may suggest that the typical policy measures based on increased controls and punishment may not lead to solving the problem of shadow economy in Poland. Importantly, the managers declare their dissatisfaction with the tax policy, State Revenue Service, government support and quality of business legislation and moreover indicate specific obstacles in running business in Poland. Therefore, it may be assumed, that the improvement in the field of tax policy, business legislations and more general in the political stability of the state may enhance the willingness to operate in the formal market.

References

Abdixhiku, L., Krasniqi, B., Pugh, G., & Hashi, I. (2017). Firm-level determinants of tax evasion in transition economies. *Economic Systems, 41*(3), 354–366. https://doi.org/10.1016/j.ecosys.2016.12.004

Ahmed, E., & Braithwaite, V. (2005). Understanding small business taxpayers. *International Small Business Journal, 23*(5), 539–568. https://doi.org/10.1177/0266242605055911

Allingham, M. G., & Sandmo, A. (1972). Income tax evasion: A theoretical analysis. *Journal of Public Economics, 1*(3–4), 323–338. https://doi.org/10.1016/0047-2727(72)90010-2

Alm, J., & Torgler, B. (2006). Culture differences and tax morale in the United States and in Europe. *Journal of Economic Psychology, 27*, 224–246. https://doi.org/10.1016/j.joep.2005.09.002

Barone, G., & Mocetti, S. (2011). Tax morale and public spending inefficiency. *International Tax and Public Finance, 18*(6), 724–749. https://doi.org/10.1007/s10797-011-9174-z

Bernasconi, M., Corazzini, L., & Seri, R. (2014). Reference dependent preferences, hedonic adaptation and tax evasion: Does the tax burden matter? *Journal of Economic Psychology, 40*, 103–118. https://doi.org/10.1016/j.joep.2013.01.005

Bobek, D. D., Roberts, R. W., & Sweeney, J. T. (2007). The social norms of tax compliance: Evidence from Australia, Singapore, and the United States. *Journal of Business Ethics, 74*(1), 49–64. https://doi.org/10.1007/s10551-006-9219-x

Buehn, A., & Schneider, F. (2012). *Shadow economies in highly developed OECD countries: What are the driving forces*? (IZA Discussion Paper). Retrieved from http://ideas.repec.org/p/jku/econwp/2013_17.html

Deskar-Škrbić, M., Drezgić, S., & Šimović, H. (2018). Tax policy and labour market in Croatia: Effects of tax wedge on employment. *Economic Research-Ekonomska Istrazivanja, 31*(1), 1218–1227. https://doi.org/10.1080/1331677X.2018.1456359

Doerrenberg, P., & Peichl, A. (2013). Progressive taxation and tax morale. *Public Choice, 155*(3–4), 293–316. https://doi.org/10.1007/s11127-011-9848-1

European Commission. (2020). *Special Eurobarometer 498. Summary. Undeclared work in the European Union.*

Fundowicz, J. (2020). *Szara strefa 2020.*

Gërxhani, K. (2007). "Did you pay your taxes?" How (not) to conduct tax evasion surveys in transition countries. *Social Indicators Research, 80*(3), 555–581. https://doi.org/10.1007/s11205-006-0007-x

Hanousek, J., & Palda, F. (2004). Quality of government services and the civic duty to pay taxes in the Czech and Slovak Republics, and other transition countries. *Kyklos, 57*(2), 237–252. https://doi.org/10.1111/j.0023-5962.2004.00252.x

Joulfaian, D. (2009). Bribes and business tax evasion. *European Journal of Comparative Economics, 6*(2), 227–244.

Kogler, C., Batrancea, L., Nichita, A., Pantya, J., Belianin, A., & Kirchler, E. (2013). Trust and power as determinants of tax compliance: Testing the assumptions of the slippery slope framework in Austria, Hungary, Romania and Russia. *Journal of Economic Psychology, 34*, 169–180. https://doi.org/10.1016/j.joep.2012.09.010

Kogler, C., Muehlbacher, S., & Kirchler, E. (2015). Testing the "slippery slope framework" among self-employed taxpayers. *Economics of Governance, 16*(2), 125–142. https://doi.org/10.1007/s10101-015-0158-9

Krasniqi, B. A., & Williams, C. C. (2017). Explaining individual-and country-level variations in unregistered employment using a multi-level model: Evidence from 35 Eurasian countries. *South East European Journal of Economics and Business, 12*(2), 61–72. https://doi.org/10.1515/jeb-2017-0017

Martinez-Vazquez, J., & Torgler, B. (2009). The evolution of tax morale in modern Spain. *Journal of Economic Issues, 43*(1), 1–28. https://doi.org/10.2753/JEI0021-3624430101

Mcgee, R. W., & Benk, S. (2019). Christian attitudes toward ethics of tax evasion: A case study. *Journal of Financial Crime, 26*(1), 74–94. https://doi.org/10.1108/JFC-11-2017-0104

Mickiewicz, T., Rebmann, A., & Sauka, A. (2017). To pay or not to pay? Business owners' tax morale: Testing a neo-institutional framework in a transition environment. *Journal of Business Ethics, 157*(1), 75–93. https://doi.org/10.1007/s10551-017-3623-2

Nur-Tegin, K. D. (2008). Determinants of business tax compliance. *B E Journal of Economic Analysis & Policy, 8*(1), 28. https://doi.org/10.2202/1935-1682.1683

Pickhardt, M., & Prinz, A. (2014). Behavioral dynamics of tax evasion—A survey. *Journal of Economic Psychology, 40*, 1–19. https://doi.org/10.1016/j.joep.2013.08.006

Putniņš, T. J., & Sauka, A. (2015). Measuring the shadow economy using company managers. *Journal of Comparative Economics, 43*(2), 471–490. https://doi.org/10.1016/j.jce.2014.04.001

Putniņš, T., & Sauka, A. (2017). *Shadow economy index for the Baltic countries 2009–2016*. Riga.

Russo, F. F. (2013). Tax morale and tax evasion reports. *Economics Letters, 121*(1), 110–114. https://doi.org/10.1016/j.econlet.2013.07.004

Sauka, A. (2008). *Productive, unproductive and destructive entrepreneurship: A theoretical and empirical exploration*. Frankfurt am Main: Peter Lang.

Sauka, A., & Putniņš, T. (2016). *Shadow economy index for the Baltic countries 2009-2015*. Riga: Stockholm School of Economics. https://doi.org/10.1017/CBO9781107415324.004

Savić, G., Dragojlović, A., Vujošević, M., Arsić, M., & Martić, M. (2015). Impact of the efficiency of the tax administration on tax evasion. *Economic Research-Ekonomska Istrazivanja, 28*(1), 1138–1148. https://doi.org/10.1080/1331677X.2015.1100838

Schneider, F. (2014). Work in the shadow: Micro and macro results. *International Economic Journal, 28*(3), 365–379. https://doi.org/10.1080/10168737.2014.936924

Torgler, B. (2007). *Tax compliance and tax morale: A theoretical and empirical analysis*. Cheltenham: Edward Elgar Publishing.

Torgler, B., & Schneider, F. (2007). *Shadow economy, tax morale, governance and institutional quality: A panel analysis* (IZA Discussion Paper No. 2563). Bonn: IZA. Retrieved from http://ftp.iza.org/dp2563.pdf

Torgler, B., & Schneider, F. (2009). The impact of tax morale and institutional quality on the shadow economy. *Journal of Economic Psychology, 30*(2), 228–245. https://doi.org/10.1016/j.joep.2008.08.004

Tourangeau, R., & Yan, T. (2007). Sensitive questions in surveys. *Psychological Bulletin, 133*(5), 859–883. https://doi.org/10.1037/0033-2909.133.5.859

Webley, P., Cole, M., & Eidjar, O.-P. (2001). The prediction of self-reported and hypothetical tax-evasion: Evidence from England, France and Norway. *Journal of Economic Psychology, 22*(2), 141–155.

Chapter 5
Conclusions and Recommendations

Abstract This summary chapter provides the reader a brief outline of the extensive research on the shadow economy in Poland, referring to the designed survey that was conducted among 454 entrepreneurs in 2017. It points out major findings from the study, puts that results into context. Finally, the authors briefly discuss observed limitations and biases that emerge when running survey research on the shadow economy. This chapter closes with drawing several prospects for the future regarding the shadow economy in Poland.

5.1 What We Have Aimed to and What We Have Found

The central focus of this book is put on tracing shadow economy determinants in Poland. With this aim we have conducted a designed survey basing on the similar survey conducted in Baltic states by Putniņš and Sauka (2015). Our survey structure and questions were designed to help for better understanding entrepreneurs' satisfaction on doing business in Poland. Our questionnaire encompassed 23 questions regarding state fiscal policy, entrepreneurs knowledge on government policies and sizes of the shadow economy in Poland, their company financial information and general performance, their attitudes and barriers in doing business, and tax morale (see Appendix A). Entrepreneurs were surveyed using telephone interviews (CATI). By definition only company owners or high level managers were questioned. Our survey sample covered 454 representative polish enterprises, which to ensure representativeness were randomly stratified using the following strata: region (voivodship), industry and employment size. Based on the survey results we constructed the Shadow Economy Index for Poland similarly to the Baltic states, following the methodology proposed by Putniņš and Sauka (2015). Moreover, relying on this survey we aimed to trace major determinants of staying in the shadow economy in Poland.

As stressed in the preceding chapters the evidence on the size and major causes of the extensive undeclared economy in Poland is relatively scattered and fragmented. During past years several trials regarding estimates of the magnitude of the shadow economic activities in Poland are traced. Before the year 2000 research on this field was highly biased by very dynamic and profound socio-economic

D. Nikulin, E. Lechman, *Shadow Economy in Poland*, SpringerBriefs in Economics, https://doi.org/10.1007/978-3-030-70524-4_5

transformation that the Polish economy was undergoing. The collapse of Soviet Block, implementation of the shock therapy, hyperinflation (in early 90s of the twentieth century), persistent structural unemployment, abrupt shifts in economic structures, widespread corruption, weak institutions and poor law enforcements combined with "post-soviet attitudes" towards doing business generated significant in size shadow economy. According to Schneider (2002) estimates in 2000–2001 in Poland the size of the shadow economy reached almost 28% of official GDP, and approximately 20% of labor force was working in the shadow. Since then onward, after the year 2000, the research on the shadow economy in Poland began to be more systematic. National Statistical Office started to complete the evidence, using module surveys on the undeclared (unregistered) work and its causes and publish in country-wide reports "Unregistered Employment in Poland in 2014" and "Unregistered Employment in Poland in 2017". The survey results are broken by gender, age, educational level, rural-urban areas, and aside from the rough estimates of the sizes of the "black labor" in includes several information on the causes of entering and then staying in the undeclared part of the Polish economy. In consecutive years these research was completed by the evidence provided in 2015 and 2016 in thematic reports developed by the Gdansk Institute for Market Economics, while in 2019 two more reports were issued by Polish Economic Institute and Institute for Forecasts and Economic Analysis. The later shows that the picture of the shadow economy in Poland is gradually becoming better studies and better understood. Aside from the evidence on the shadow economy provided by national agencies, we trace some empirical research developed by scholars. The most recent studies may be found in works of, inter alia, Mróz (2016, 2018, 2019), Buszko (2017), Adair (2020), Baklouti and Boujelbene (2020), Bashlakova and Bashlakov (2020), Bednarski (2019), Lyulyov and Moskalenko (2020), Nchor (2020) or Nikulin (2020).

Our research and its findings add to the picture on the shadow economy in Poland. Relying on the survey conducted we contribute to the state-of-the-art by providing more detailed evidence on the shadow economy determinants. Bearing in mind the fact that our survey was conducted exclusively among entrepreneurs, these results demonstrate the business-side view on the shadow economy, while it ignores the workers views, perceptions and opinions. By convention, our survey examined the business climate in Poland, entrepreneurs view, opinions and attitudes, however—indirectly, basing on respondents answers we conclude about the major causes driving people to go and stay in the shadow economy. Our results, although evidently biased due to the method used (direct surveys—see brief discussion in the next section), limited sample and geographic coverage, they allow for several conclusions regarding factors influencing the shadow economy. As clearly stated from the answers received a huge share of respondents demonstrate their dissatisfaction from the state tax and—more general—fiscal policy. They perceive it as an overburden and significant "justification" regarding their relatively low tax morale. In their views the tax and fiscal system are "unjust" and "unfair", which—in their opinion, justifies undeclared economic activities. This is quite common among entrepreneurs in Poland to feel the unfairness of the tax system, which combined with low tax morale, poorly functioning labour market, relatively low (insufficient) income and unemployment, constitutes a perfect ground for going into shadow economy. Tax burden and low tax morale evidently drive high propensity to get involved in undeclared economic activities. In we add to these high entrepreneurs' dissatisfaction regarding quality of business legal frameworks and poor state support for entrepreneurial activities (see Chap. 4), that explains relatively large shadow economy in Poland. On the other hand, if look at consecutive results from the survey we observe that our respondents they generally disagree with the statements that tax avoidance or bribery are tolerated in Poland. Our respondents also reply that in their opinion cheating on tax is not justified behaviour, while in another two questions they state that tax rates, tax administration, trade and custom regulation, as well as business licencing and permits or instability of state regulations are one of the major obstacles in doing business. In short surveyed entrepreneurs feel that high administrative burden and general overregulation are highly disadvantageous for their entrepreneurial activities. Entrepreneurs when asked about corruption, anti-competitive practices and political instability, around 70% of them claimed these three elements as significant obstacle in doing business. By convention, our survey did not encompass direct question regarding undeclared economic activities. Still received answers signal that t Polish entrepreneurs perceive business climate in Poland as not very favourable and they diagnose various obstacles. Their responses, although not direct, they clearly suggest what are the major drivers of the extensive shadow economy in Poland – tax burden and low tax morale, excessive state regulations and their instability, poorly designed tax administration, corruption.

Apparently, for the last years, the size of the shadow economy in Poland is not actually shrinking. According to Polish Institute of Economic Forecasts and Analyses estimates since 2015 the unobserved (undeclared) production on Polish economy is growing in absolute terms (from 243 PLN billions[1] in 2015 to 294 PLN billions on 2019). Still, according the same estimates, it has to be acknowledges that due to activities undertaken by the state tax authorities but also several legislative changes, between 2014 and 2019 we observe drops in share of gross domestic product generate in the shadow from 19.5% of GDP in 2015 to 17.2% on 2019. Polish Institute of Economic Forecasts and Analyses in its analysis also reports that three major channels of generating the shadow economy in Poland are recognized, and these are: (1) tax evasion/tax fraud regarding value added tax that significantly reduced state tax revenues; (2) cash settlements aimed at reducing labour costs and bureaucratic burdens and (3) underreporting of sale and turnover figures, which is mainly observed in case of legally operating enterprise, usually small or micro-enterprises operating in services, which—to a large extent, refers to unreported to official statistics, remunerations paid to workers "under the table".

[1] In market prices.

5.2 Limitations and Further Research Directions

Asking about the size and determinants of the shadow economy is always a tricky question. Researchers intending to deal with these issues are permanently exposed to a significant number of constrains and limitations, while obtained results suffer from different biases, weaknesses and are prone to open criticism. Both direct and indirect methods have certain advantages and disadvantages, and the last may heavily violate the whole picture emerging from the study.

In this study we have deployed a survey method to collect data, information and entrepreneurs "sentiments and feelings" on major determinant of the shadow economy in Poland. Designed sample surveys, a microeconomic approach for empirical research, rely on voluntary replies of entrepreneurs, and although broadly adopted for country-wise analysis of undeclared economic activities, they are affected by various inherent flaws (Schneider & Buehn, 2017). Sample survey results suffer from different biases, like, geographic bias, sectoral bias, respondents bias, limited-sample bias; henceforth they often lack representativeness and—what is even more urgent, the results are highly sensitive to respondents included in the survey. Moreover, survey data usually are not collected on annual, regular basis which violates in-time comparability of obtained results. Another, very significant biases and survey-based research limitations arise from the very human nature and personal features of respondents. Apparently, obtained responses depend on whom is surveyed, how surveyed people perceive economic reality, what is their economic and legal knowledge, what are their expectations and prospects, but also their personal attitudes, morale and social norms they accept. Finally, the general precision and accuracy of survey results greatly depend on the respondent's willingness to tell the true story about business they run. For instance, estimating the amount of undeclared work or income paid "off record" from responses in direct questionnaire seems a challenging task as far as most entrepreneurs usually hesitate to confess to fraudulent behaviours being afraid of formal consequences from authorities. This is one of the reasons why survey methods tend to underestimate sized of the shadow economy. Henceforth, the reliability of these answers can be easily questioned. Adding to these limitations listed above, differences in understanding or interpreting open questions in the survey by respondents, difficulties in capturing feelings, expectations and attitudes in limited number of questions significantly reduces the conclusiveness of survey results violating true estimates of the sizes of shadow economy, undeclared incomes and labour. More concerns regarding the sample survey adoption for estimating size and examining determinants of shadow economy arise if we bear in mind that most of direct surveys are small-scale intensive surveys that are usually conducted in specific and purposing selected localities and companies (Lemieux, Fortin, & Frechette, 1994; Williams, 2006; Williams & Windebank, 2001, 2005). While small-scale surveys tend to be often qualitative studies it is barely possible to gain country-wide picture of the sizes, determinants, causes and within-country distribution of the shadow economy. Using direct, country-wide survey approach is relatively rare and in such cases indirect methods are preferred (see, for instance, works of Schneider & Enste, 2013; Mauleón & Sardà, 2017; Fedotenkov, 2019). Finally, sample survey results on shadow economy lack international consistency and comparability. In past empirical evidence we may trace several works presenting results of similarly designed surveys conducted in different countries, compare for instance in Pedersen (2003), Feld and Larsen (2009) or Haigner et al. (2013). In 2007 European Commission undertook several attempts to run similar surveys among member countries to obtain cross-country comparable results on shadow economy. However they found that implementing the designed survey in consecutive countries met several barriers like e.g. wording of the questionnaire relying on country-specific cultures and national language specificity. Still, despite several significant flaws of direct approaches used in shadow economy analyses, certain advantages of this method can be admitted. The first and the main advantage is that this method offers the researcher, candid responses, detailed information about the structure of the shadow economy, it allows tracing entrepreneurs' sentiments on business climate, their morale towards, e.g. tax system. Still, this method is very sensitive to the survey is conducted and questions formulated, but well designed and well-structured questionnaires may provide extensive knowledge on business perceptions, business realities, motives for going into shadow and socio-economic features of those shadow workers in a country. Sample surveys also demonstrate relative versatility; they can be tailored for specific needs of the research and adjusted to local context and conditions that will allow more fully understand the shadow economy phenomenon.

Bearing in mind all the shortages and limitations in deploying survey method for research on shadow economy, conclusions shall be draw carefully and results treated with caution. The study in question shall be well contextualized, supported by extensive discussion regarding social, economic and legal aspects that will allow putting obtained results in certain framework to fully understand the phenomenon of the shadow economy, but also allow capturing all the effects of the shadow economy that emerge simultaneously in labour market, in production and monetary income structure.

5.2.1 So What Comes Next?

Our study was conducted on a limited sample of companies in 2017. The questionnaire used in the study, although well-designed and structured, it did not allow capturing all aspects of the shadow economy in Poland. Using company-based micro approach had certain advantages, like for instance it enabled to talk directly to the entrepreneurs instead of households. The construction of the questionnaire, at least to some extent, discovered entrepreneurs' attitudes towards tax system in Poland, and gave some critical remarks about the general business climate and prospects. Still our study, as mentioned above, is prone to respondents sincerity and voluntarity to take part in the survey. Apparently, a consensus has emerged that to build more complex picture of the shadow economy in Poland, more extensive in its merit and scope direct surveys shall be implemented. Needless to claim that an ideal solution for more propounding understanding of the shadow economy size and determinants, would be implementation of the large-scale longitudinal studies to achieve temporal and spatial comparability. Additionally enlarging the scope of direct studies would increase the representativeness of the method, which potentially might facilitate detecting emerging some sensible and logical patterns in respondents answers to allowing to develop more comprehensive picture. Surely, several modifications in the questionnaire itself, improving data collection method and confidence in validity of the research, would also be advantageous. Another useful modification to the original survey would be more detailed geographical and sectoral breakdown to ensure more balanced results.

Finally, if only possible, to ensure the highest accuracy and validity of the research on the sizes and causes of the shadow economy, researchers should combine several methods, but also their adoption in various countries and periods would benefit in building the holistic picture of the phenomenon. So far, the empirical is relatively scattered, fragmented, and usage of different methods brings—sometimes radically, different results. Hopefully, improving research methods and enlarging their scope will allow for better understanding why people work in the shadow economy, what is their motivations and what share of their disposal income comes from undeclared economic activities.

5.3 Prospects for the Future

In June 2014 Poland joined the United Nation Global Compact programme to fight more effectively against corruption and shadow economy. The emerged Global Compact Network Poland aims to publish on annual basis country reports regarding countering the undeclared economy and the corruption in Poland. As we read in the report "Countering Shadow Economy in Poland 2018" the major aim of the programme is "*(…) to create a unique platform for collaboration between the private sector and state institutions to counter the shadow economy, corruption, and tax fraud in industries most exposed to economic crimes. The strategic objectives entailed improving the quality and effectiveness of the public administration, strengthening the enforcement of laws and regulation and promoting the dissemination of responsible corporate practices*" (Global Compact Network Poland, 2018). The programme is designed to "*counteract corruption and diminish barriers for economic and social development related to the existence of shadow economy (and/or related to criminal activities)", while its strategic targets include: "improving the quality and effectiveness of public administration; improving the quality and enforcement of laws and regulations; promotion, implementation and dissemination of practices of responsible and sustainable corporate policies.*[2]" Under this programme, on annual basis, the report on the scale of the shadow economy, certain

[2] Extracted from: https://ungc.org.pl/wp-content/uploads/2018/07/Countering-Shadow-Economy-poj-www.pdf (accessed: November, 2020).

risks in business functioning, and problems that business owners have to face in Poland is published. The programme concepts originates from the 10th Principle of the UN Global Compact according to which "Anti-Corruption—Businesses should work against corruption in all its forms, including extortion and bribery[3]", and this is directly linked with the UN Sustainable Development Goals 2030,[4] and especially with goals 8, 9, 10, 12, and 16.

In Polish Economic Institute policy paper 7/2019 "The shadow economy in Poland" we trace developed scenarios regarding reduction of size of the shadow economy in Poland in forthcoming years—until 2023. According to developed three scenarios—optimistic, moderate and pessimistic assuming that the size of the shadow economy is reduced by 1 pp per year or 1.5 pp per year until 2023. If the optimistic scenario with the 1.5 pp of annual drop in the shadow economy size is considered by 2023 state budget shall receive approximately 87.4 PLN billion more from taxes, which would mean that by 50% of actual tax loses are converted into tax revenues. Needless to say that state policy efforts and strategies entirely depend on the efficiency and effectiveness of planned actions. Changing entrepreneurs' mindsets, perception and attitudes toward doing business in Poland seems to be one the most crucial point in future actions.

References

Adair, P. (2020). Non-observed economy vs. shadow economy and informal employment in Poland: A range of mismatching estimates. In *Comparative economic studies in Europe* (pp. 249–278). Cham: Palgrave Macmillan.

Baklouti, N., & Boujelbene, Y. (2020). A simultaneous equation model of economic growth and shadow economy: Is there a difference between the developed and developing countries? *Economic Change and Restructuring, 53*(1), 151–170.

Bashlakova, V., & Bashlakov, H. (2020). The study of the shadow economy in modern conditions: Theory, methodology, practice. *The Quarterly Review of Economics and Finance* (in press).

Bednarski, M. (2019). Social determinants of the shadow economy in the small and micro-sized enterprise sector from the local perspective. Conclusions of empirical research. *Problemy Polityki Społecznej. Studia i Dyskusje, 44*(1), 87–100.

Buszko, A. (2017). The impact of the shadow economy on small and medium sized companies in Poland. A barrier or an opportunity for growth? *International Journal of Business and Economic Development (IJBED), 5*(2).

Fedotenkov, I. (2019). Corporate labour share of income and the shadow economy: A cross-country analysis. *Applied Economics Letters, 26*(4), 302–305.

Feld, L. P., & Larsen, C. (2009). *Undeclared work in Germany 2001–2007—Impact of deterrence, tax policy, and social norms: An analysis based on survey data*. Berlin: Springer.

Global Compact Network Poland. (2018). *Countering shadow economy in Poland, GCNP 2018*. Retrieved from https://ungc.org.pl/wp-content/uploads/2018/07/Countering-Shadow-Economy-poj-www.pdf

[3] https://sdgs.un.org/goals

[4] https://sdgs.un.org/goals

Haigner, S. D., Jenewein, S., Schneider, F., & Wakolbinger, F. (2013). Driving forces of informal labour supply and demand in Germany. *International Labour Review, 152*(3–4), 507–524.

Lemieux, T., Fortin, B., & Frechette, P. (1994). The effect of taxes on labor supply in the underground economy. *The American Economic Review*, 231–254.

Lyulyov, O., & Moskalenko, B. (2020). Institutional quality and shadow economy: An investment potential evaluation model. *Virtual Economics, 3*(4), 131–146.

Mauleón, I., & Sardà, J. (2017). Unemployment and the shadow economy. *Applied Economics, 49*(37), 3729–3740.

Mróz, B. (2016). Online piracy: An emergent segment of the shadow economy. Empirical insight from Poland. *Journal of Financial Crime, 23*, 637–654.

Mróz, B. (2018). Shadow economy in a turbulent environment: Evidence from Poland. *Journal of Money Laundering Control, 21*(3), 328–339. https://doi.org/10.1108/JMLC-08-2017-0034

Mróz, B. (2019). Bridging the tax gap in Poland. *International Journal of Economic Policy in Emerging Economies, 12*(1), 49–61.

Nchor, D. (2020). Shadow economies and tax evasion: The case of the Czech Republic, Poland and Hungary. *Society and Economy*.

Nikulin, D. (2020). Tax evasion, tax morale, and trade regulations: Company-level evidence from Poland. *Entrepreneurial Business and Economics Review, 8*, 111–125.

Pedersen, S. (2003). *The shadow economy in Germany, Great Britain and Scandinavia. A measurement based on questionnaire surveys* (The Rockwool Foundation Research Unit, Study, 10).

Putniņš, T. J., & Sauka, A. (2015). Measuring the shadow economy using company managers. *Journal of Comparative Economics, 43*(2), 471–490.

Schneider, F. G. (2002). *The size and development of the shadow economies of 22 transition and 21 OECD countries* (IZA Discussion Papers, No. 514). Bonn: Institute for the Study of Labor (IZA).

Schneider, F., & Buehn, A. (2017). Estimating a shadow economy: Results, methods, problems, and open questions. *Open Economics, 1*(1), 1–29.

Schneider, F., & Enste, D. H. (2013). *The shadow economy: An international survey*. Cambridge: Cambridge University Press.

Williams, C. C. (2006). Evaluating the magnitude of the shadow economy: A direct survey approach. *Journal of Economic Studies, 33*(5), 369–385.

Williams, C., & Windebank, J. (2001). Reconceptualising paid informal exchange: Some lessons from English cities. *Environment and Planning A, 33*(1), 121–140.

Williams, C. C., & Windebank, J. (2005). Eliminating undeclared work: Beyond a deterrence approach. *Journal of Economic Studies, 32*(5), 435–449.

Appendix A: Survey Questionnaire

Entrepreneurs' Satisfaction with Business Climate/Informal Entrepreneurship in the CEE, CIS and Sweden

My name is ... from ... . We are conducting a survey aimed at understanding entrepreneurs' satisfaction with entrepreneurship climate in Poland. The main interest of the study is to find out how various policy initiatives implemented within the country and entrepreneurs satisfaction with business climate influences entrepreneurial behaviour, including tax avoidance.

I would like to emphasize that we are only interested in your expert opinion and in no way are we indicating, for instance, that your company is involved in any type of tax avoidance activities.

The interview will last approximately 15 min. We guarantee 100% confidentiality as neither your name nor your company's name will appear in the data analysis. Data will be analysed using a computer program without any reference to the data source. If you are interested, we can also send you the summary of the survey results once the survey is complete.

If respondent hesitates or says 'no':

This survey is very important to foster the knowledge about the entrepreneurship in Poland. By participating in this survey you are helping to improve such knowledge. All your answers will be 100% confidential and no one will be able to track you or your company. Moreover we are interested in your expert opinion and what you say will be attributed to the industry or your competitors, not your firm.

D. Nikulin, E. Lechman, *Shadow Economy in Poland*, SpringerBriefs in Economics, https://doi.org/10.1007/978-3-030-70524-4

Questionnaire Form

External Influences

Q1. Please evaluate your satisfaction with the performance of the State Revenue Service with regards to tax administration.

1	2	3	4	5
Very unsatisfied	Unsatisfied	Neither satisfied nor unsatisfied	Satisfied	Very satisfied

Q2. Please evaluate your satisfaction with the government's tax policy in Poland.

1	2	3	4	5
Very unsatisfied	Unsatisfied	Neither satisfied nor unsatisfied	Satisfied	Very satisfied

Q3. Please evaluate your satisfaction with the quality of business legislation in Poland.

1	2	3	4	5
Very unsatisfied	Unsatisfied	Neither satisfied nor unsatisfied	Satisfied	Very satisfied

Q4. Please evaluate your satisfaction with the government's support to entrepreneurs in Poland.

1	2	3	4	5
Very unsatisfied	Unsatisfied	Neither satisfied nor unsatisfied	Satisfied	Very satisfied

Q5. Tax avoidance is tolerated behaviour in Poland.

1	2	3	4	5
Completely disagree (Entrepreneurs do not tolerate involvement in tax avoidance)	Disagree	Neither agree nor disagree	Agree	Completely agree (Entrepreneurs highly tolerate involvement in tax avoidance)

Q6. Bribing is tolerated behaviour in Poland.

1	2	3	4	5
Completely disagree	Disagree	Neither agree nor disagree	Agree	Completely agree

Government Policy and Amount of Informal Business

Q7. Please estimate the degree of underreporting business income (in percent) by firms in your industry in 2016_______ % and in 2015 _______ %.

Q8. Please estimate the degree of underreporting number of employees (% of actual number of employees) by firms in your industry in 2016_______ % and in 2015 _______ %.

Q9. Please estimate the degree of underreporting salaries paid to employees by companies in your industry (for instance, if in reality an employee receives EUR 400, but the reported salary is EUR 100, then underreporting is 75%; if EUR 400 and EUR 200, then underreporting is 50%). Firms underreported actual salaries by approximately ____ % in 2016 and ____ % in 2015.

Q10. On average, approximately what percent of revenue (turnover) did firms in your industry pay in unofficial payments to 'get things done' in in 2016_______ % and in 2015 _______ %.

Q11. When other firms in your industry do business with the government, approximately how much of the contract value would firms typically offer in unofficial payments to 'secure' the contract? (year 2016)_____%

Q12. In some industries, in addition to registered companies such as yours, unregistered enterprises also operate but do not report any of their activity to authorities. In your opinion, what percentage of your industry's total production of goods/services is carried out by unregistered enterprises in 2016?_____% in 2015? _____%

Q13. For a typical company in your industry, what would you say is the approximate probability (0–100%) of being caught if the company were to:

(a) underreport its business income? ______%
(b) underreport its number of employees? _____%
(c) underreport the amount it pays to employees in salaries? _____%
(d) make unofficial payments to 'get things done'? _____%

Q14. If a company in your industry were caught for deliberate misreporting, what would typically be the consequence to that company?

Nothing serious	A small fine	A serious fine that would affect the competitiveness of the company	A serious fine that would put the company at risk of insolvency	The company would be forced to cease operations
1	2	3	4	5

Company/Performance/Value Creation

Q15. What is the approximate percentage change in your operating profit, turnover and total employment in 2016 compared to 2015?

	1. Operating profit	2. Turnover	3. Total employment
Change (increase or decrease in %) as compared to 2015. For example: +20%, −15%, 0 (no change)			

Q16. Approximately, what was the operating profit of your company in 2016?
EUR __________

Q17. Approximately, what was the turnover of your company in 2016?
EUR __________

Q18. Approximately, how many employees are currently employed in your company (full time equivalent, including you)?
__________ employees

Q19. In which year did your company start operation?
Year________

Q20. What is the main activity (i.e. sector) that your company is engaged in?

☐ Manufacturing
☐ Wholesale
☐ Retail
☐ Services (please specify________________________________)
☐ Construction
☐ Other (please specify________________________________)

Q21. What is the place in *(insert country)* where:

(a) your company is located (headquarters/main office):
(place: town/city)____________________Postal code__________________________
(to be provided by vendor in case respondent can not answer)

(b) your company does most of its business:
(place: town/city)____________________Postal code__________________________
(to be provided by vendor in case respondent can not answer)

(c) your company is registered:
(place: town/city)____________________Postal code__________________________
(to be provided by vendor in case respondent can not answer)

Attitudes/Tax Morale/Barriers to Business

Q22. For each of the following statements, please indicate on a scale of 1–5 whether you agree (1 means you completely disagree, 5 means you completely agree):

	Strongly disagree	Disagree	Neither/ nor	Agree	Strongly agree
(a) Businesses such as yours contribute a lot to growth of the polish economy and society in general	1	2	3	4	5
(b) Companies in your industry would think it is always justified to cheat on tax if they have the chance	1	2	3	4	5
(c) Being a member of the local community is important to me	1	2	3	4	5

Q23. As I list some factors that can affect the current operations of a business, please tell me if you think that each factor is No Obstacle, a Minor Obstacle, a Moderate Obstacle, a Major Obstacle, or a Very Severe Obstacle to the current operations of this establishment.

	No obstacle	Minor obstacle	Moderate obstacle	Major obstacle	Very severe obstacle
(a) Tax administration	0	1	2	3	4
(b) Tax rates	0	1	2	3	4
(c) Trade and custom regulation	0	1	2	3	4
(d) Business licencing and permits	0	1	2	3	4
(e) Functioning of the judiciary/courts	0	1	2	3	4
(f) Uncertainty about regulatory policies	0	1	2	3	4
(g) Corruption	0	1	2	3	4
(h) Anti-competitive practices of other competitors	0	1	2	3	4
(i) Political instability	0	1	2	3	4

Appendix B: Survey Sample

Employment level	No. of companies in the sample
1–5	240
6–10	199
11–20	5
21–40	6
41–60	3
101–150	1

Sector	No. of companies in the sample
Manufacturing	85
Wholesale	35
Retail	57
Services	228
Construction	49

Region (voivodship)	No. of companies in the sample
Lower Silesia	38
Kujawy-Pomerania	31
Lublin	19
Lubuskie	13
Lodz	34
Malopolska	41
Mazovia	79
Opole	14
Podkarpacie	18
Podlasie	2
Pomerania	16

D. Nikulin, E. Lechman, *Shadow Economy in Poland*, SpringerBriefs in Economics, https://doi.org/10.1007/978-3-030-70524-4

Region (voivodship)	No. of companies in the sample
Silesia	50
Swietokrzyskie	12
Warmia-Masuria	15
Wielkopolska	47
West Pomerania	25

Source: Own elaboration based on company survey study